中國夢‧廣東故事
　　——創新的廣東

作者　陳翔 CHEN XIANG

The China Dream :
Guangdong Story - Innovation

Editors: Li Jie, Wang Ning

Published by Guangdong People's Publishing House Ltd., China

www.gdpph.com

First published 2017

Printed in the People's Republic of China

The China Dream: Guangdong Story- Innovation/ Chen Xiang and translated by Feng Honglin

ISBN 978-7-218-11891-8 (paperback, 1st edition)

Preface

Located in southern China, Guangdong Province is the first region in China to implement the reform and opening up, and it is also one of the most affluent areas nationwide. The Pearl River, China's third largest river, runs across the whole province. The Pearl River Delta is an alluvial plain flushed by the Pearl River. After nearly 40 years of rapid development, it has already become one of the most important city groups of China. The Hong Kong Special Administrative Region, and the Macao Special Administrative Region adjoin to Guangdong Province. With the natural geographical relations and the same cultural background, they constitute China's unique Guangdong-Hong Kong-Macao Greater Bay Area—a world-class vigorous economic and cultural area.

For nearly 40 years of rapid development, Guangdong has been playing a leading role in innovation, spurring the rapid development of new growth drivers. There are many rapidly grown-up enterprises in Guangdong, such as Huawei, Tencent, and UMi, which have become important engines of Guangdong's new economy development. Huawei and Tencent are now widely known in China. We try to approach such enterprises and their employees, to find the "secret" of the most innovative and cutting-edge development in Guangdong.

Guangdong has been the most dynamic foreign trade area in China since ancient times. And Guangzhou has been a commercial city through the ages, as well as an important interconnecting city alongside the "Maritime Silk Road". Foreigners from all over the world travel across major cities in Guangdong everyday, sightseeing, attending business meetings, studying or visiting friends. In Guangzhou, there are a large number of foreigners from Europe, America, Southeast Asia, the Middle East, Africa and other places, doing business here everyday. They ship back clothing, fabric, seafood, electrical appliances or glasses; foreign trade is booming. In the Shenzhen Special Economic Zone ports, people and vehicles travelling between Hong Kong and Shenzhen are always lined up. Foreigners living here for many years gradually adopt and merge into customs and culture of Guangdong, and regard Guangdong as their "second home". Meanwhile, tens of millions of workers from other provinces live in Guangdong, especially in the Pearl River Delta, where they work in factories, earn money to support their families, and try to realize their own dreams and ambitions. Whether foreigners or migrant workers, they are all practitioners, promoters and witnesses of Guangdong's reform and opening up. We conduct close observation of their work and life to record their ups and downs.

Ten years ago, the per capita income in the Pearl River Delta had already reached the level of that of moderately developed countries, and it is moving towards high-income phase. But the embarrassment is that in the eastern, western and northern parts of Guangdong Province, there are still large number of underdeveloped rural areas, and some places are even in extreme poverty, which distresses successive provincial governments. The government is determined to carry out large-scale " poverty alleviation" action, and vows to lift all peasants of impoverished areas out of poverty in three years, and promote common prosperity in these parts of Guangdong like the Pearl River Delta.

As the most populated, dynamic, and developed province that has been spearheading reform and opening up, recent practices in Guangdong are full of strength and sweetness. We go into it, and hope to find and record those breathtaking, touching and impressive stories of the development in Guangdong these years. Those people and those stories constitute a glaring part in the glittering development of the new era in Guangdong.

Through these stories, you can see diligence and endeavors of Guangdong people in the process of modernization. Through the perspective of Guangdong, you can see great efforts of Chinese people in realizing the China dream of the great rejuvenation of the Chinese nation.

總序

　　廣東省位於中國南部，是中國最早實行改革開放的區域，也是目前中國最富庶的地區之一。中國的第三大河流珠江穿越廣東省全境，由珠江沖積而成的珠江三角洲在經過近四十年迅速發展後，已經成為中國最重要的城市群之一。香港特別行政區、澳門特別行政區與廣東省毗鄰，天然的地緣和一脈相承的人文情緣，構成了中國獨有的粵港澳大灣區──一個世界級活躍的經濟人文區域。

　　和中國其他地區一樣，在經過長達近四十年的高速發展之後，廣東面臨產業轉型升級轉變發展動能的重任，創新驅動成為推動此輪變革的重要抓手。廣東省內有許多近年來快速成長起來的新型企業，比如華為、騰訊、有米科技，它們成為廣東新經濟發展的重要引擎。華為和騰訊，以及它們的「老闆」任正非和馬化騰，在中國幾乎家喻戶曉。我們試圖走近這樣的企業及其員工，找到廣東創新驅動最前沿的發展「密碼」。

　　廣東自古以來是中國對外商貿最活躍的地區，廣州是千年商都，是「海上絲綢之路」重要的節點城市。來自世界各地的外國人每天往來於廣東省內各大城市，他們或旅遊觀光，或商務會議，或求學訪友。在廣州，每天大量來自歐美、東南亞、中東和非洲等地的外國人在這裡做生意，他們把這裡的服裝、布匹、海產品、電器或者眼鏡託運回國，外貿做得紅紅火火。在深圳經濟特區口岸，進出香港和深圳的車輛、人流常常排成長龍。長年生活在這裡的外國人，在生活習俗和文化上逐漸接受並慢慢融入廣東，廣東成為他們的「第二故鄉」。與此同時，更多的數千萬計的來自中國內地的普通勞工常年生活在廣東尤其是珠江三角洲地區，他們在工廠裡「打工」，憑藉「打工」掙下的錢養家餬口，並試圖實現自己的人生夢想。無論是外國人還是農民工，他們都是廣東改革開放的實踐者、推動者和見證者。我們近距離觀察他們的工作和生活，記錄他們的喜怒哀樂。

珠江三角洲地區早在十年前人均收入便已達到中等發達國家水平，正邁向高收入階段。但令人尷尬的是，在廣東省的東、西、北部仍有大片生活並不富裕的農村，一些地方甚至還處於貧困狀態，這讓廣東省歷屆政府頗感頭痛。政府下決心開展大規模的「扶貧」行動，並發誓要在三年後讓所有貧困地區的農民擺脫貧困，力促粵東西北地區與珠江三角洲地區走向共同富裕。

作為人口最多、經濟最活躍、總量最大、地處改革開放前沿的省份，廣東近年的實踐既具有力量又讓人感到溫馨。我們深入其中，希望通過我們去發現去記錄，在廣東發展這些年中，那些或動人心魄或充滿溫情或飽含人性的故事。那些人，那些事，終將構成廣東新時期史詩般發展歷程中炫目的一環。

通過這些故事，人們可以看見，在現代化進程中廣東人的奮發圖景；透過廣東，可以看見中國人民為實現中華民族偉大復興的中國夢的奮鬥歷程。

Contents

When Factories and Villages Encounter the Internet

A Penguin Who
Changes the World

Pony Ma's Three Crises

In September 1987, Zorn, a German professor, attended a technology symposium in Beijing. After a series of conditioning, he managed to connect the Institute of Computer Application Technology of Beijing with the Computer Center of Karlsruhe University by the computer.

On 14th September, Zorn and Wang Yunfeng, a Chinese professor, drafted an e-mail together, saying "Across the Great Wall we can reach every corner in the world," and "This is the First Electronic Mail from China to Germany", of which the title and content are both written in English and German. It is the famous e-mail later known as "Across the Great Wall, to the World".

▲ On the evening of 14th September 1987, in the Institute of Computer Application Technology of Beijing, a dozen people gathered around a big Siemens Computer, among whom we found Professor Wang Yunfeng and Professor Zorn.

In addition to the professors, Wang Yunfeng and Zorn, there were 11 participants from China and Germany who also signed on the e-mail.

But there was a problem in the e-mail server CSNET that one bug in the PMDF agreement led to a dead cycle, which delayed the successful

▲ The first e-mail sent from China.

sending of that e-mail. After consultations, they received confirmation from the CSNET Information Center that there was always the problem, especially when the phone circuit worked badly. Professor Zorn's assistant Michael Finken, staying in Beijing and Gerd Wacker, staying in Kurlsruh, worked together to make up with software for the unstable signal confusion, overcoming many obstacles such as working jet leg. Seven days later, on 20th September, that e-mail finally reached Germany, crossing half of the globe.

By now, the 45-year old Pony Ma, who comes from Shantou, Guangdong Province, has created TENCENT for over 18 years. Dating back to a few months ago, 11th November 2016 was the 18th anniversary of TENCENT. On that day, Pony Ma, together with the CEO office staff, sent out WeChat red packets to current employees, former employees, outsourcing employees and company service personnel, totaling at 30 million yuan.

But that was not the climax. Pony Ma later announced a decision that they would give each current employee 300 TENCENT stocks. Calculated by TENCENT's stock price of 200 HK dollars per stock, the bonus they planned to give out this time was worth 1.5 billion yuan.

Of course, TENCENT's stock price is a mythic legend. On 16th June

▲ "QQ's Father" Pony Ma has an appearance of Confucian elegance and is of gentle and modest character.

2004, TENCENT Holding was officially listed, opening on that very day at 4.375 HK dollars, which has accumulatively increased by 250 times twelve years later.

Because of the development of mobile phones, China has become the country where the internet including mobile internet is most widespread in the world. In Pony Ma's concept, during the last five years, TENCENT has evolved through a closed environment into an open environment and has become a real interconnected eco-system. " Some former internal business lines which did not perform well have been cut, sold or given away, only the most nuclear telecommunication and digital content is retained, including the 'internet+' which is being promoted now. The so- called ' + ' is to fully cooperate with other enterprises."

Judged from its market value of more than 230 billion dollars, TENCENT is now the biggest internet company in Asia. This entrepreneur, who calls himself as a typical " programming ape (programmer)" and who never thought of setting up a company, behaves very modestly on many occasions, even when he is with close friends or the family. "In these 18 years of TENCENT, what I more frequently say is thank you. Thank you, all my colleagues."

In fact, he is holding in hand a stupendous user group and a giant business empire. The number of monthly active users of TENCENT's WeChat and QQ has respectively reached 806 million and 899 million, while in 2016, the total population of mainland China was only 1.38271 billion.

His appearance is of Confucian elegance and he looks very gentle. But this "QQ's Father" always has a very strong marketing ability accompanied by very deep crisis awareness. When commenting on his experiences of business development, the media always use such words as awestruck, creative and open, etc.

According to Pony Ma, TENCENT met three biggest difficulties in its development history.

The first difficulty occurred at the financing period of its initial stage. At the beginning of development, TENCENT team went through the toughest time of biding failure and lacking money to buy servers to meet the overgrowing number of users. But this kind of difficulties also forced TENCENT team to think about how to generate blood to support its growth from very early on.

The second difficulty was the competition with MSN. " Other people all thought at you were to die, the only question was when. But we survived. Our products were made to meet Chinese users' habits better than foreign products." It was because TENCENT made a lot of modifications by taking China's internet condition and Chinese users' habits into consideration that it won the war against MSN.

The third obstacle occurred five years ago before WeChat was born, when TENCENT was faced with a very big pressure since Sina Weibo turned from social media to social network.

Of course, the biggest crisis in TENCENT's history should be the "3Q War" in 2010. The disputes between QIHU 360 and TENCENT had been a long story originating from the "jostles" of their "star products" in 2012. On 27th September 2010, QIHU 360 issued its newly developed "privacy protector" which focused on collecting information about QQ's invasions of users' privacy. Soon afterwards, QQ immediately pointed out that 360 explorer was suspected to make promotion through pornographic websites. On 3rd November 2012, TENCENT announced that all the computers with 360 software installed should stop running QQ software, and users were allowed to log in QQ only when they had unloaded 360 software, forcing users to make an "either-or" selection.

On their own interests, these two companies started a series internet wars from 2010 to 2014 and ended up with lawsuits.

They sued each other for three times with QIHU 360 lost in the end, among which QIHU 360's monopoly charge against TENCENT caught most attention. On the morning of 16th October 2014, the Supreme People's Court decided that TENCENT's QQ did not occupy a dominant position in market and rejected QIHU's appeal, maintaining the judgment

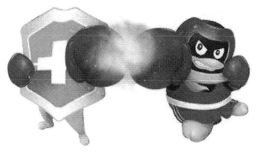

▲ Memory of the war between TENCENT and 360 remains fresh in netizens' mind.

of the first trial.

On 5th December of the same year, Pony Ma announced that TENCENT would enter into a preparation period of strategic reformation which would last for half a year. He said: "'monopoly' is an irritating charge. In most cases, it is an imagined enemy, something that does not exist. In the 90s of the 20th century, we could see that in our IT industry Microsoft was the company which was most criticized and charged against in the name of monopoly. When the era of internet came, what problems was Microsoft faced with? We saw a lot of new companies still able to stand out. It was hardly possible that all creators and all entrepreneurs thought that they had no future. What chance was left when Microsoft might enter many areas and occupy the first position in many industries? But we all witnessed what actually happened in the following years. We saw the rising of not only Google but also eBay. In particular, Google was a very powerful company which could do everything, getting involved in all internet product lines. Still we saw the rising of Facebook. When Facebook started to think that there was no other threats to challenge its position in the market of social network and interpersonal relationship, we saw the rising of a new form—Weibo.

Pony Ma said with a little grievance, "So, we can see that a lot of the so-call monopoly companies are still faced with huge crises when the industry is continuously experiencing reforms. That is to say, in the industry of which the value changes rapidly, there is not a single company can rest easy. So, to challenge Alibaba, Baidu and TENCENT which are called three big mountains, the best way is not to build up a similar platform to create monopoly but to follow the trend to form a good industrial chain. Only that can be called a good way. "

"Looking back, I could gain a lot of reflections on it, but I do not want to indulge myself in all the disputes, what I expect more is to go forward and look forward." Pony Ma said, that dispute pushed TENCENT to make reformation and transformation more firmly. "We hope this is a prudent, thorough and complete transformation."

Soon thereafter, TENCENT sold the business lines such as searching and e-commerce one after another in the form of investment, and focused on the basic connecting service of internet public affairs.

A Magic Path from Imitation, to Public Enemy, and to Industry Leader

When commenting on TENCENT's development path, IT commenters concluded: "TENCENT has been created for 18 years, walking through a magic path from imitation, to public enemy and to industry leader."

In 1984, Pony Ma was brought by his parents to Shenzhen. He received secondary and high education in Shenzhen Middle school and Shenzhen University. After graduation, he worked for a telecommunication company in Shenzhen for 6 years, and then started a business with his middle school and university classmates and one peer from telecommunication industry, 5 persons in total. At that time, the total number of netizens in China was only 3 million.

▲ Penguin is TENCENT's brand image.

In the year of 1999, nearly nobody could be definitely sure about how big an imagination could the internet development bring to people. At the very beginning, internet was most often applied as technology and was accessed by only a few people. Such a thing that only existed at technical level could hardly inspire people's imagination. Under such background, in the dilemma of buying a house or starting a business, it was obviously Pony Ma's foresight of internet and IM that made Pony Ma resolutely and determinately discover internet and develop QQ. Even Lei Jun also refused to invest in TENCENT at that time.

You can say that Pony Ma made QQ by accident since it was a side product of telecom products. But that opinion could not explain why soon thereafter QQ could surpass OICQ which was IM's ace product in a very short time in terms of server storage and personal images, etc. Those products may seem very ordinary to us now, but they were great creations at that time, just as WeChat that we are using now.

Earlier or later, QQ might not have succeeded. But it grasped the first bonus of the initial stage of China internet, which laid a solid foundation for TENCENT's being listed later on and even for the present social empire.

At the preliminary stage of the start-up period, TENCENT made right actions at several critical moments.

▲ TENCNET Logo, penguin image at the center.

The first was the operator's bonus. Though QQ gained a lot of users at the initial stage, how to earn money was obviously a big problem at that time. After all, the capital market still held a very conservative attitude toward internet and there was no such a saying as market dream rate. The financing passing industry chain was not mature at that time and enterprises had not enough financial support to say that, "We do not think of profit for the moment." At that moment, QQ grasped the life-saving straw, the operator, and took advantages of that opportunity to turn around.

At that time, SP business, which could be said as the earliest way for internet enterprises to make money, saved QQ's life to a large extent. Without those SP businesses, QQ might have been sold at 1 million yuan. With that income, QQ could not only support its own operation, but also laid a good foundation for its being listed later on. At that time internet enterprises still could not easily get capital investment under the condition that they had not made profit yet. While doing SP, QQ itself performed relatively well. On one hand, QQ developed functions of value-added capacity such as membership and QQ show, on the other hand, QQ started to issue Q currency which is up to now the only hard currency that can rival telephone card. SP business declined in the end, but QQ grasped the critical opportunity and got rid of the predicament at this round.

The second was the explosion period of PC applications. In 2005, after TENCENT was listed, QQ had nearly become a gigantic product. It was an explosion period of desk software such as TTPlayer, Baofeng Video Player, Xunlei, input method, etc. which were listed as must-installed softwares for a computer. Under such condition, TENCENT, by using the powerful resource distributing channels of QQ, started to develop a series of similar products such as QQ Video Player, QQ Music, QQ Explorer and QQ Input Method, etc. Though QQ was criticized by the whole industry, we can see it clearly that many of TENCENT's current horizontally developed products are based on what were made at that round, such as the newly independent QQ Music and the QQ Explorer which has ranked among the top explorers in market share. In addition, it was also during this period that QQ beat MSN. It might not be known to many that MSN used to have a bigger market share than QQ at its golden age.

八卦　　　浏览资讯　　　看杂志

游戏　　　　　　　　　　　　听音乐

Show自己　　　　　　　　　　听广播

看节目　　　　　　　　　　　玩游戏

Shopping　　　养宠物

▲ TENCENT products.

TENCENT also took advantages of the opportunity to launch web portal, which was under the shadow of three big web portals at that time. But TENCENT web portal fought hardly by using QQ resources such as mini pop-ups and tips etc., and finally managed to become the fourth biggest web portal after Sina, Sohu and NetEase. That's strategically meaningful to TENCENT. In addition to certain speech right, the web portal also laid a foundation for the upcoming QQ Live and QQ Sports. Web portal advertising was internet enterprises' second important income resource following value-added service. The foundations that QQ had laid at this period not only provided a space for future development, but also constructed a strategic defense.

The third was the game window. Chen Tianqian's Shanda pushed the internet into an era of " digging gold with excavator". Internet entrepreneurs finally discovered another fastest and most profitable way of making money in addition to value-added service and advertising. TENCENT luckily grasped what has become the most important revenue resource up to now. But at the beginning, it was not so easy for TENCENT to enter into the domain of games. The first few games did not stand out selling well, and were even unknown to most people. It was not until TENCENT discovered games of playing cards that the platform developed by TENCENT quickly defeated Ourgame and became the hottest platform, in which QQ's social relationship chain found its true value. And it was also from that time that TENCENT started to realize the natural compatibility of social contact and games. In view of the success of card games, TENCENT continued to launch some other successful games such as DNF, then CF, to current LOL. Now TENCENT has acquired half of market share in the domain of games.

The most important was that TENCENT grasped the chance at the explosion period of social network. The sudden rising of Facebook inspired many internet companies, and a number of websites grew up very rapidly, including the former Xiaonei Web and Happy Web. At that time, the social characters of those websites could even be compared to QQ as horse and horse. But QQ had a most important Ace—QQ Space. I remember reading a statistics that even at its best time the market share and user share of Renren Web (the former Xiaonei Web) of social platform was not at the same level as that of QQ. Games such as stealing vegetables and moving cars were very hot at that time, but the rapid response of QQ Space won the users immediately. Until now, many people will still ask a question: " Why there is no Facebook in China? " In my opinion, QQ ' s blocking actions against Renren Web and Happy Web by using QQ Space completely destroyed the dream of having Facebook in China. The rapid development of QQ Space did not only help QQ transform from IM to an integrated social platform, but also laid a foundation for the upcoming Feeds advertising. The Feeds advertisements in QQ Space are considered as the best quality resources by many enterprises.

What is the Next Creation that Will Influence the World?

At the initial stage of starting a business, leadership was totally out of Pony Ma's consideration, and what was most important to him was to keep the company surviving. He said: "Both of my parents never expected a nerd like me could be able to start up a business. So the first step was to find partners. They could make up for my shortcomings."

Among the partners he had found, Xu Chenye, Zhang Zhidong, and Chen Yidan were his middle school or university classmates, and Zeng Liqing was his former colleague. They all had different strong points which were well complementary to each other. What Pony Ma needed to do was to "make full use of each one's strong points and balance each one's opinions." He was not a bossing CEO and he did not decide all things of management. At the early

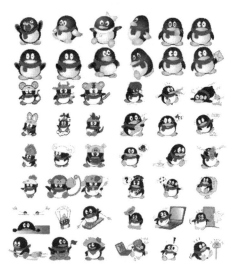

▲ The penguin puts on hundreds of thousands of images, playing different roles.

stage, the partners often sit together for two or three hours with one pot of chicken rice on each one's hand, discussing business affaires at the table. Many company's important decisions were made on such occasions. Eating chicken rice was a symbol of TECENT's partnership culture. Even when the partners gradually stepped out from the first line management, they still maintained very good interactions without making any disharmonious voices or events. Chen Yidan's explanation was that the partners were from similar family backgrounds, which resulted in the fact that they were of similar characters. They were all relatively gentle and prudent and can accept negotiation mechanism instead of pursuing personal heroism.

But since the internet keeps changing every second, how can TENCENT Empire keep being creative? That is what Pony Ma must face.

In 2010, all the people were contending for ship tickets to get aboard the mobile internet. That was a war of either to die or to survive. The

▲ The old building of TENCENT headquarter.

companies such as Baidu and 360 were deemed to be faced with a risk of being left behind since they failed to bring out products that had real influential power. TENCENT's condition was also not very good, with Weibo aiming at the social network and QQ bearing a heavy history burden when transforming from PC to mobile. Pony Ma confessed that it was the biggest crisis they had ever encountered.

At that time, three TENCENT internal teams engaged in the development of revolutionary products. The one who solved the mobile phone terminal problem would be the winner. Finally, QQ Postbox team developed a client end product which could quickly receive and send e-mails through mobile phones. So quickly that the user would think it was not an e-mail. That product was what we called WeChat later. Allen Zhang, its developer, became the father of WeChat.

In TENCENT, they were used to the fact that competitors might be their colleagues. Pony Ma did not consider it as a problem; instead he even thought that good internal competition was very necessary. "You will work hard only when you are beaten by yourself. And it ensures that the company will not lose some big strategic chances."

In 2013, interviewed by CCTV at a dialogue show, Pony Ma claimed that they had got a standing ticket for the mobile internet. In June 2016, he said, the ship had already pulled in before we could sit down, and it was to set foot on a new land. A new round of technological innovation represented by the artificial intelligence was the future trend, on which internet giants including TENCENT were working hard at a faster pace.

Witnessing the contest between AlphaGo and human, Pony Ma and his team all felt very excited. They were eager to do something at this new age of technology after so many years of dreariness.

Storing 3.5 million applications and distributing 2 million per day, AppQQ version 7.0 will add a robot function based on AI and iCloud, so that users can call a taxi without loading Didi Taxi in the future. TENCENT will make more research and development based on AI, and will make it open to more partners.

Even so, Pony Ma still does not know what will be the next creation that will influence the world. "Every big reformation is accompanied with the change of device. The whole eco-system becomes different in consequence of the popularity of smartphones. New changes will occur in application situations as VR and AR devices become more and more popular in the future.

Ever since he went to school, Pony Ma always loved astronomy which had not direct connection with his business but did affect how he thought to some extent. He said: "The Love for astronomy

▲ The new building of TENCENT headquarter.

would make you feel so small that we may always be an accident in the universe. That would make you become more optimistic and think that it is not a big deal whatever you are facing."

Artist Allen Zhang and WeChat

Today, Chinese people's dependence on WeChat is almost extreme, which is also the excellent achievement of TENCENT Empire in the second decade of the new century.

Pony Ma recalled that at that time there were three teams making the WeChat product. It was reasonable to let another former business group of QQ to develop IM for mobile phones at this new chance. In addition, they were also developing mobile QQ, of which the original product structures were unreasonable, and then we quickly made adjustments to integrate all products, such as news and games, which were separated in PC and in mobile phone.

"Another one was the QQ Postbox Team at Guangzhou who has been engaged in mobile office since very early. So we started to consider whether we could develop an App in QQ Postbox to let every employee use mobile phone mail very conveniently. That team was required to develop a mobile mailbox. It was this team of

▲ The WeChat icon.

5 or 6 people that changed the mobile mail system into WeChat. So WeChat was actually a mail system for quick short mails, of which the server in the back was the former postbox team. It only took one month or so for the team to produce a prototype. This team led by Allen Zhang has

very strong product ability."

" It did not arouse much attention when WeChat was newly launched. The real reasons for its popularity were as below. The first one was its voice function which similar foreign products lacked of, and it made the App become very popular in a short time. The second one was the matching with phone contacts. The first step was to link it with QQ contacts so as to make it survive. But the input of phone contacts would introduce many high-end users and increase the connection."

As a key person, Allen Zhang looks dark skinned and is a middle age man who likes playing golf. He is also commented by many people as "playing the role of an artist" most of the time and "he takes products as the artworks he creates." During these 17 years, Allen Zhang kept making self-replacement and self-upgrading. The Foxmail sold at 12 million yuan many years ago was a commercial failure rather than a product success. It was much more a pity that he lost a huge commercial opportunity in contrast with that money. That was Allen Zhang 1.0 associated with key words as product and technology. At the early stage of WeChat, he upgraded the tool to a platform, turned the simple requirement of serving users to guide their sentiments, and finished the second upgrade.

In the fall of 1998, Zhou Hongyi was introduced to Allen Zhang in Guangzhou for the first time. He saw this programmer who was already of some renown sitting with a dozen people in a small and old office surrounded by thick smoke. Seeing Zhou Hongyi, Allen Zhang put out the cigarette held in his hand and walked toward him with a poker face. The

Foxmail developed by Zhang, which already had 2 million users, was the shareware that had the biggest group of users in China, while Zhou Hongyi was only a vice supervisor of the Research and Development Center of Founder Soft at that time.

Zhou Hongyi said, Foxmail had no commercial mode at that time, for which he always criticized Allen Zhang, and he suggested making profit by adding advertisements. Allen Zhang replied him by asking why he should do that. Feelings were all that he required. Each time, such kind of arguments was ended by Allen Zhang's longstanding silence. "How could such a person have developed WeChat?" Zhou Hongyi was confused.

When Foxmail was at its golden age, TENCENT only had a hundred thousand users, and many people considered mailbox as a bigger domain than social contact. When Pony Ma and Charles Zhang were excitedly looking for venture capital and making commercializations, Allen Zhang was often reading users' letters alone late at night. His hands would not leave the keyboard, always clicking the down arrow, watching letters flowing in front of his eyes one by one with none of them staying more than one second. In Allen Zhang's eyes, Foxmail had

▲ The login image of WeChat— a lonely person facing the blue planet Earth.

become a huge burden. Countless people were urging him to run forward every day, while the huge fame and user number did not bring him with any economic and social benefits.

One year later, Allen Zhang decided to sell Foxmail to a not very well-known internet company Boda. The night after the news was released, he wrote a letter full of sad sentiments, in which he described Foxmail to be an artwork he elaborately made. "From soul to appearance, I can count every detail and every story of it. In my heart, it has a soul because every section of its codes has my awareness when I was creating it. I suddenly feel an impulsion to recall my decision. "

Artist Allen Zhang was always a lonely creator. In the past, he was walking freely on the broad runway until there occurred two obstacles-commerce and profit. While countless sharewares such as Maxthon, TTPlayer and Supper Rabbit were hit off the way, Allen Zhang luckily entered another runway. He was then only 31 years old, and many people thought that his personal legend seemed to end at that point.

That summer, Baidu was listed in NASDAQ. All thought there must be something wrong with their eyes, shocked by the fact that Baidu's stock was rising sharply from the issue price 27 dollars to 122.54 dollars with a boom of 354%. People had realized the power of capital and commerce, while Allen bought a car with the acquisition money that Boda gave him and went to Tibet where he was always longing for.

"How should I put it, this guy, is too naive." said Zhou Hongyi. Such the entrepreneur who was famous for his being crafty and fighting in the commercial world commented on Allen Zhang who was even one year older.

Missing the first climax when internet was hitting NASDAQ, Boda started to decline. In 2005, Allen Zhang and Foxmail were sold to TENCENT as a package. Taking charge of QQ Postbox, Allen Zhang made it become the biggest mail service provider surpassing Net Ease mailbox. He just proved his product ability one more time.

In many times, the powerful ones were always businessmen, while most artists had to rely on businessmen's financial support and could not control their own lives. Foxmail brought Allen Zhang great fame and a very unstable destinies. He was always surrounded by businessmen. He made friends with them, and even wanted to learn from Microsoft how to make commercial operation, but he never set foot on commerce. At last, most of his friends who had both product-making and commercial talents all succeeded, such as Lei Jun, Zhou Hongyi, Pony Ma, and even the journalist Li Xueling who had interviewed him.

Someone commented that Allen Zhang was always following the trend, but he was not in it. From a programmer to a product manager, he learned to control his products, but he could never control users. But the generous destiny gave him a third chance, and this success was so great and was coming so fast.

Zen Ming was one of the 13 original team members. He said that nobody, including Allen Zhang, knew what WeChat should be made into at that time, not to mention that half of those members were interns who had zero experience. Their original target was to make it fast and stable, which was the same as what Allen Zhang had in mind when he was making Foxmail, a pure thinking of making tools. If Allen Zhang's product concept was stuck at that level, what he would make would be merely an acceptable chat tool.

Some colleagues compared Allen Zhang to a director who wanted to film a perfect block buster. It was not that he could not accept advertising implantation, but that he could not stand obvious implantation which would destroy the perfection. Wu Yi, who used to be the Assistant General Manager of Tenpay, described that when he met him for the first time three years ago, Allen Zhang was thinking about how to couple WeChat and commerce through payment: "He does not reject perfect cooperation, such as QQ Music, QQ Postbox and payment."

At the early stage of WeChat, Allen Zhang was responsible for product, while the commercial rules such as how to lead in the third party merchants and how to expand online and offline buisiness were all the responsibilities of Dai Zhikang, the vice president of TENCENT E-Commerce, and even the payment part was made to be done by the Tenpay team. At the end of 2012, Luo Yihang, the starter of Pingwest, wrote an article saying that the reason why WeChat was commercialized too slowly was due to the internal disputes between Zhang and Dai.

A series of events, such as Dai Zhikang's dismission, WeChat Payment's integration into WeChat after being separated from Tenpay, and the independence of WeChat business group, happened hereafter. You could consider them as the choice that Allen Zhang had made—since it was inevitable to commercialize WeChat, then WeChat team should take the lead in making the commercialization. At the same time, it also indicated that the TENCENT management represented by Pony Ma and Liu Zhi had made their choice that they chose to delegate

▲ Allen Zhang created WeChat after suffering from longstanding loneliness, perfectly combining the artist's feelings and the commercial profit making mode.

Allen Zhang with a full charge of the commercialization.

Within the company, he took the control power over commercialization, and to the public, he tried to build up a new system to handle the relationship between art and commerce. For example, in TENCENT there used to be 120 projects queuing to be adopted into WeChat, while what WeChat required was to run them for one and a half months and then to make selection according to the statistics.

"WeChat includes the commercial actions such as launching what kind of functions and taking in what kind of cooperative partners as part of the product, while to many people, product is part of commerce." One of TENCENT's senior management told the journalist that you could interpret it as a commercialized value and an artist's methodology.

Even until today, TENCENT's commercial strategies are considered as relatively conservative. One insider gave his comments to the journalist

▲ WeChat payment increased common users' trading speed.

that facing commercialization, Allen Zhang was experiencing an adapting process from escaping and attempting, to leading. He was never absolute. He never promised anything that he was not able to do. He might even avoid talking about something that he was able to do.

The commercialization of WeChat shoulders the big dream of the whole TENCENT's transformation. For the moment, it is divided into three steps: the value-added service, e-commerce and O2O. Now only the first step is completed, while official accounts can realize the latter two steps simultaneously. Zen Ming says that WeChat will open more entrances and will provide the flow inlet expected by all merchants in the future.

Commenters used to conceive WeChat as merely a flow leading tool. But now by means of official accounts, WeChat connects TENCENT's powerful online marketing ability with offline business and has built up an enormous online + offline eco-system, in which all kinds of small ecosystems such as e-commerce, O2O, and healthcare service will emerge. The difference between WeChat and QQ can be compared to that between the real economy and the virtual economy, the latter is only less than 7% of the former.

In the past, Allen Zhang was used to stand behind businessmen, now he has come to the

▲ Allen Zhang's team.

first line, following Pony Ma's path—being a product maker and a commercial leader at the same time. But commercial interests are huge and complicated. So we can imagine that Allen Zhang will still choose to keep silent in a long period of time.

Pony Ma recalled that when WeChat was newly launched, the operators became very nervous at the fact that nobody texted and people seldom made calls. "I would constrain you, and many countries around the world would make many rules to constrain you. But that was irresistible. I was always telling them that you should not be worried and you would definitely be benefited. Your voice service declined but your internet flow increased. How would that damage your profit? The growth was hard to predict. Till last year, statistics was growing faster than that of former voice service. They are now assured that the relationship between us is like that between fish and water. "

"Trumpchi",
Legend!

The Ambition of Entering America and a Car Named GS8

The first Trumpchi car rolled off the production line in Guangzhou seven years ago. At that time, in the second decade of the new century, the private car market was getting bigger and bigger in China.

Now, this auto brand, ranking the sixth in terms of sales volume in China, will be the first Chinese brand that is allowed to be exhibited in the main exhibition hall on the North American International Auto Show at the end of 2017. Observers believe that its major challenge of entering the American market is the high cost related to tests and to meeting the requirements of the highest safety & emission standard in the world. "The rules in the U.S. are too much stricter than that in China."

Guangzhou Automobile Group (hereinafter referred to as GAC) is performing better and better. In 2016, it was listed in Fortune Global 500 for the fourth consecutive year, ranking the 303rd, up by 59 compared to last year.

All around the world, its self-creative ability has become a salient representation of its regional competiveness. Today, the number of high-tech enterprises in Guangdong Province has ranked at the first position in China, achieving some targets of transforming old energy consumption to the new. The success of Trumpchi, the self-own automobile brand of

Guangzhou automobiles, is the most shining page on the performance report on the automobile industry of Guangdong Province.

Up to now the total investment has accumulated to 13 billion yuan since 2005 when GAC planned to creat a self-own brand. GAC has built up a domestic first-class research and development center and a world- class plant producing vehicles and engines, and has launched its self-own brand Trumpchi. In the 2015 Report on Chinese New Vehicle Quality issued by J.D.Power, Trumpchi was the quality champion of Chinese brands for the third consecutive year, ranking the 8th along with GAC TOYOTA. As for its sales volume, Trumpchi has witnessed a jumping growth since it was launched into market in 2011 when the figure was 17 thousand, and 116 thousand in 2014. The sales volume of Tumpchi in 2015 was 190 thousand increasing by 63% year on year, while that of China vehicle market was only 4.7%. The total annual sales revenue was 17.7 billion yuan, and the monthly sales volume of GS4, the first Trumpchi SUV, managed to rank the top 3 among all SUVs of the whole China. It is said that a "1513" strategy has been included in the 13th Five- Year strategic planning initiated and implemented by GAC. The "1" key point is to develop self-own brands with the whole group's efforts and to realized jumping development of self-

▲ The automation level of production line for Trumpchi reaches at 60%.

own brand business.

In 2016, Trumpchi made a " double breakthrough" of both sales volume and brand. On January 2017, Trumpchi kept on growing by riding on the momentum of last year's good performance. In January, the total sales volume of Trumpchi was 46273, increasing by 60% year on year, which ranked top among the domestic auto makers, pushing Chinese local brands to a higher level. Among the Trumpchis, the sales volume of GS8, the "flagship luxury huge 7-seat SUV" newly launched for only three months, was 9418 in January, greatly increasing for three consecutive months.

The single-month sales volume of GS8 was 9418, standing out along with Highlander and Edge in the sales market of median and large SUV. It was the first time that a Chinese local brand held a strong stance when fighting with its joint venture rivals face to face. It was also the first time in Chinese auto history that GS8 succeeded in the price range of 160000 to 250000 yuan where Chinese local brands had never reached before.

If keeping such high developing speed, GS8 is hopefully to surpass Highlander and Edge, and to become the top 1 in its market segment. The GS8 sales at the moment are also running toward this "small target". Once realized, it would undoubtedly be recorded in Chinese auto history, inspiring all the people who have been working hard for the rising of Chinese automobiles for more than 30 years and confirming their confidence in it.

Not only that, the hot sales of GS8 enabled Trumpchi to get rid of the embarrassment of walking by one leg. The hot-sale auto types increased from one to two, making the product structure approaching a reasonable status, and the price deviations of different types were further enlarged. It also pushed the sales weight of Trumpchin in GAC to increase from last year's 22.38% to 27.55%, increasing by 5% and approaching 30%.

Marked by GS8 hot sales, Trumpchi is leading Guangdong auto industry to transform from being "Made in Guangdong" to "Created in Guangdong" and to upgrade the reputation of "Made in Chia" from product to brand. In the near future, following the gradual development of its overseas strategies, especially its official landing in the US market in 2019, Trumpchi will also help to expand the reputation of "Chinese Brand" from the Chinese market to the global market. "Trumpchi will become the leading brand of Chinese autos. The annual sales plan of 1 million vehicles will be realized before the originally expected year 2020." On the eve of the 2017 North American International Auto Show, Yu Jun, Vice President of GAC Execution Committee and the General Manager of GAC Motor,

▲ CS4

made that prediction with great confidence.

The emergence of GS8 is definitely not accidental and not of any luck. It is the result of Trumpchi's insistence on high-end development strategies, on positive exploitation, and on international standard. From the original GA5, to GS5 & GS4, the price of Trumpchi is always the highest compared to that of all other local autos. The average unit price is even higher than that of some joint venture brands. Before the arrival of GS8, the average unit price of GS4 was around 140 thousand yuan. With the advent of GS8, the unit price of Trumpchi autos is directly increased to a brand new level of 200 thousand yuan, wining a broad strategic space for the upcoming auto types.

After being launched, the appearance design of GS8, which is "super hard and powerful", receives positive responses from both the media and consumers. However, the excellent appearance design is only one of the reasons why GS8 has gained such an excellent success. Trumpchi also provides "assured driving control at any terrains", "large seven-seat space", "new horizon and intelligent interconnection" and advanced quality with competitive price, which precede customers' expectation.

Since its being launched, GS8 has obtained nearly a hundred domestic and international awards such as "Annual China Brand SUV", "Annual Best Performing Large SUV", "Top 10 Highly Recommended New Autos 2016", and "Annual Most Popular SUV", and has been widely admired by the media and auto authorities, gaining good harvests of both sales and reputation.

▲ The new model of GS8 is of striking appearance.

At the same time, according to J.D. Power SM (IQS), Trumpchi brand has been the top 1 of China brands for four consecutive years. The quality of Trumpchi automobiles surpasses that of most joint venture products, and consumers' common trust becomes the internal factor for the hot sales of Trumpchi products.

In the market trend of consumption upgrading, brand attraction and product quality are playing more and more critical roles in the competition among auto enterprises. GS8 is fully loaded with the creative achievements made by Trumpchi in the domains of R&D, design and manufacturing.

In the Chinese market, an auto company obtains a market passport for the whole price range, once it can break into the market of prices range from CNY 200 to 250 thousand. TOYOTA and HONDA obtain a good share in the global mainstream vehicle market because of the hot sales of Camry and Accord. The success of GS8 is of milestone significance to Trumpchi, which makes it possible for Trumpchi to compete with Acura, Infinite and Cadillac, and enables it to fulfill its potentials in the market segments of Class B, A+, A and A0.

Trumpchi is not the first Chinese brand who insists on high-end product, and of course will not be the last one. In the past decade, Chinese auto has met ups and downs, and the reality has proved that only the insistence on "brand upwards" and "keeping on positive R&D" is the right direction that Chinese local auto brands should be heading toward. Entering all middle and high-end markets of severe standards, to some extent, is to exhibit one's competitiveness to all customers.

GS8 has successfully upgraded Chinese local brands and even "Made in China" to a new high level, which is not a result of inflated pricing and not of verbal boast, but of actual orders and real sales figures. In the price range of 160 to 250 thousand yuan, it has received 40 thousand orders within 3 months with a sales volume of 9418 per month. We cannot say that it will not be surpassed by newcomers, but at least it is unprecedented.

The representatives of "Made in China" are Huawei in the technology domain, and Gree and Haier, the leading enterprises in the household appliance industry. In order to complete the mapping of "Made in China", auto enterprises must be included. A nation's image of manufacturing industry can only be set up around the world with its auto enterprises to sprint at full speed and to break the tape. In addition to the British,

American, German, Japanese and Korean brands, the world auto industry is also going to embrace Chinese brands which are rising up as represented by Trumpchi.

There is No Shortcut to Technological Innovation

Walking along the production line of Trumpchi, one may have an illusion of being in a science-fictional world: robots are waving their giant arms to make precise welding and assembling, unmanned carts are delivering all kinds of parts to their exact positions; empty auto bodies are entering from one end one by one, and brand new Trumpchi cars are coming out from the other end in succession…

The connotation of the word "Trumpchi" is explained by Zeng Qinghong, President of GAC, as being lucky and happy. He says: we want to convey luck and happiness to all of our customers by our self-own brand cars.

But it is not easy to realize that beautiful wish. "When Trumpchi was newly launched, my faith almost collapsed." Wu Song has always been in charge of the production and sales of Trumpchi products. When other GAC joint venture brands, such as GAC HONDA and GAC TOYOTA, were earning a lot of money for the company, the baby Trumpchi had been faced with huge deficits for several consecutive years. He was irritated at the market's innate distrust on the quality and performance of self-own brands. What really toasted him upside down was his colleagues' mocking as "You will be sent to work on Trumpchi if you do not work hard."

Faced with the huge pressure brought by the dominance of joint venture brands in the market, self-own brand cars were predestinated not be able to win a position in the domestic market which was the biggest in the world and was developing at a high speed? Under such condition, they initiatively lowered the production and sales target of Trumpchi, but they insisted on keeping high product quality. Zeng Qinghong said that quality was the best guarantee for the success of Trumpchi brand. There was no such a brand without quality. The first task of Trumpchi was to ensure its quality. He firmly believed that Trumpchi would succeed.

After years of efforts, overcoming the most difficult period for self-own brand autos to be accepted by the market, Trumpchi started to become more and more popular for its excellent quality and high performance-cost ratio. From January to October in 2016, the accumulated sales volume of the whole series of Trumpchi is 296 thousand, increasing by 126% year on year. The total sales volume of this year was expected to

▲ The engine production line of Trumpchi.

surpass 360 thousand, which would rank Trumpchi among the tops of Chinese auto brands in terms of development speed and profit making level.

When GAC self-own brand autos were newly launched, nearly nobody, including insiders and ordinary consumers, had faith in them, because at that time, Trumpchi had no experts, no money and no technology. It was mocked as a "3 NOs" company. The most critical problem was that GAC lack of vehicle design and R&D abilities. How could a self-own brand be made without the ability of vehicle design?

But it is out of everyone's expectation that GAC should have built up an international advanced auto research institute by investing more than 10 billion yuan. The number of research personnel has increased from around 30 to more than 3000. Now in the institute, we can find a dozen advanced laboratories of vehicle, power assembly, and new energy, etc., a trial production factory covering welding, coating, final assembly and machining, and special trial runways for auto calibration. The institute is equipped with an ability of making R&D, trial production, and testing for vehicles and key parts. All those factors are providing Trumpchi with outpouring momentum for its development. "GAC Research Institute is able to develop five new auto types per year." said Zhang Fan, Vice President of GAC Research Institute.

Growing from zero vehicle developing ability to a current capacity of launching a batch of auto types, developing a batch, and reserving a batch, now GAC Research Institute has launched a series of auto types covering the whole range of auto products. "The success of GAC Research Institute and the improvement of self-own brand auto design ability indicate that there is no shortcut to technological innovation. We must walk forward step by step." says Zeng Qinghong.

"The development of self-own bran autos will not be roses all the way, but I always believe that in the future self-own brand autos will surely take the lead in China's auto market, and Chinese self-own brand autos will definitely become popular around the world." As the one who has witnessed and participated in the whole rising process of China's auto industry, Zeng Qinghon denotes that not only ordinary passenger vehicles and commercial vehicles but also new energy autos are promising.

There are always great expectations for new-energy autos, but the research and development path is very tortuous. "Our feelings are very complicated when we see little obvious advancements or face even dead

▲ Zeng Qinghong, General Manager of Guangzhou Automobile Group Co., Ltd.

ends after investing a huge amount of money." says, Zeng Qinghong. But he believes that new-energy autos can definitely be involved in the lives of thousands of families in the future as ordinary autos do for the moment.

The Story of the " R&D Foreign Brain" Marco

Marco Mario Gilardi's office is located in the GAC Research Institute at Hualong Town of Panyu Disctrict of Guangzhou. As the Chief Egineer, Marco has participated in the whole process of the development of GAC's first self-own brand car "Trumpchi", playing a very important role. Huang Xiangdong, Director of GD Automobile Engineering Association and former President of GAC Research Institute, describes that Marco's importance to the development of Trumpchi is like a leg to a table: "A table has four legs, and if one is missing, a trouble comes along that the table will not be able to stand up."

There are many other " foreign brains" like Marco in Guangdong Province. In recent years, priority is put on the foreign expert introduction which is part of the talent introduction project of Guangdong Province. According to the statistics reported by the Provincial Statistics Bureau, the number of foreign experts introduced into mainland China in 2014 and 2015 is respectively 132.1 thousand person-time and 129.9 thousand person-time, weighting 21.3% and 20.8% in the whole country. The number of hired foreign experts is ranking the first in China. These foreign experts contribute their powers to the innovation-motivated development of Guangdong with their enthusiasm and specialized knowledge.

At the beginning of "the 11th Five-Year Plan" period, Guangzhou proposed the plan of producing self-own brand autos. In July 2006, GAC built up the GAC Research Institute based on the former Guangzhou Automobile Technology Center, which was especially responsible for the development of Gaungzhou self-own brand autos. Huang Xiangdong, former professor of the South China University of Technology and Vice President of GAC, took up the post as the first president of the Institute.

The newly established GAC Research Institute had only four technology departments except three service departments. There were only a little more than 30 research personnel, most of whom were young people without experience. That made it very difficult to develop their selfown brand cars. So they considered the task of recruiting talents as their Marco, Chief Engineer of GAC Vehicle Integration top priority. Just at that time, Huang Xiangdong met his old friend Marco who he had not seen for 25 years at Turin, Italy.

"I had met some people who came from Guangdong in a cooperation project of GAC

▲ The China Dream:Guangdong Story. Innovation

and FIAT, and with closer observation, I found Huang Xiangdong!" when talking about their second encounter, Marco said it was a fortune.

In the 80s of the 20th century, Huang Xiangdong used to work in FIAT Research Center, when Marco was newly enrolled in FIAT after graduation. They worked in the same office. When they met again, Marco had been working in FIAT for nearly 30 years, while Huang Xiangdong had also been focusing on the auto industry, working as professor at SCUT, Vice Presindent of GAC, and then being designated to build up GAC Research Institute.

At that time, FIAT had business lines in China, and Marco often came to China on business trips. He had a very good impression on China. After Huang Xiangdong had described the ideas on developing self-own brand autos to him, he often came over to make "a cameo appearance", giving young researchers some technical guidance.

"GAC Research Institute was very small at that time, and they only rented one floor from SCUT as their office. Marco often came over to make 'guest guidance' totally out of his willing to help his old friend and former colleague." Huang Xiangdong has admired Marco's personal quality very much since he was working in Italy.

In December 2007 and April 2008, after several rounds of difficult negotiations and detail consultations, GAC and FIAT signed the technology transfer contracts of engine and of chassis platform. Marco was designated to the company, taking charge of the business with GAC. At that time, the idea of making self-own brand autos was quite clear and had

▲ GAC-FIAT Viaggio

entered actual preparation stage. They were in greater want of talents. Huang Xiangdong considered directly hiring Marco to work in GAC.

"Are you willing to work in GAC?" Huang Xiangdong asked Marco, who replied him with his usual humor: "What took you so long to ask me this question since we have been cooperating with each other?"

Leaving FIAT where he had been working for 29 years and leaving his wife alone in Italy, Marco said he had "found passion and target here." Faced with Huang Xiangdong's invitation, Marco hesitated though he thought it might be a good idea. Marco had been working in FIAT for nearly 30 years, holding a relatively high post, and he should have been able to work until retirement without any big changes. And at that time his two daughters had grown up and were working overseas. If he also left, his wife would be left alone in Italy. It was not an easy decision for him to make. FIAT also tried to retain him. "Somebody told me that FIAT had already introduced Chrysler Company, and if you want to have some overseas working experience, you can go to Chrysler Company." Besides, compared with Chrysler, GAC at that time was only a small company which was little known internationally.

But Marco finally chose GAC, which was hard to understand for many people. But he described it as "a choice following his heart." "I suddenly realized that I had spent 29 years in FIAT and I did not want to continue." Marco thought that he needed a new challenge and a turning point. "It was not bad if I continued to work in FIAT routinely, but I always believed that I could also make a good career in China if I was good enough."

"I had a very good impression on GAC during previous cooperation, because I had found passion and target here." When talking about the choice he made at that time, Marco said that he was touched by GAC's atmosphere and the personnel's passion. "Having known about GAC's personnel, I increasingly found that the young people here had great enthusiasm to do it well. The management members here also had strong determination to establish the biggest and strongest leading enterprise in the auto industry. So I became more and more impressed and interested by the people and affairs here." Besides, Marco was well prepared because of the knowledge accumulated from his past working experience: "I wanted a chance to start from zero and to turn over a new page. But it was not a zero

▲ GAC Research Institute at Hualong Town, Panyu District, Guangzhou.

start in another sense, because I had acquired very good experience from the past."

Starting from nothing, not even chassis, GAC Research Institute developed its first self-own brand. Marco' s importance was like an indispensable leg to a table. In November 2009, Marco joined GAC, when the working condition was still very poor, even the laboratory had not been built up yet, while the target of Guangzhou at that time was to welcome guests by using Guangzhou self-own brand cars during the Asian Games which would be held in Guangzhou in 2010. Relevant Guangzhou government officers considered it as "the No.1 Self-Innovation Project of Guangzhou."

At first, many people thought it was a "mission impossible". After joining it, Marco started to lead the young team to set off toward the target. He was mainly responsible for the development of vehicle integration and chassis. In order to finish the tasks smoothly, Marco hardly took a rest even at weekends, and he also needed to make experiments outside Guangzhou. "We conducted vehicle experiment in Xiangyang, sand field experiment in Baotou, and ice and snow experiment in Heilong jiang."

▲ Trumpchi assisted in Guangzhou Asian Games.

Of course, all the members of his team worked at the same tempo. "Not only me who worked overtime at weekends, so did many team members. I worked, they worked. It was not me who was pushing them; instead it was them who were pushing me." It was of course not a small difficulty to develop the first self-own brand auto in two years. As Huang Xiangdong put it, they started from nothing, not even chassis. But, this team overcame many difficulties. In September 2010, eve of Guangzhou Asian Games, GAC's first self-own brand car "Trumpchi" finally came off the production line, realizing the "self-own brand auto dream" which Guangzhou people had been making for years.

As planned, 500 Trumpchi cars, as official automobiles for the 16th Asian Games, provided services to distinguished guests from Asia and all around the world. "Marco was involved in the whole process." said Huang Xiangdong.

"At the beginning, our team was very weak without any experience and was in want of someone to guide. At that critical moment, we needed backbones. And Marco was one. Huang Xiangdong says that when the team has grown up step by step, he is still needed as a backbone. "The whole team can perform well only when its core can perform well, and Marco is one of the most excellent members of the core team." In September 2014, the Chinese Government awarded Marco the highest honor for foreigners—the National "Friendship Award". In April 2015, Marco was successfully included in the fourth national " Recruitment Program of Thousand Foreign Experts". But, Marco does not consider himself as a "mentor". "I never teach them anything. I just work with them." says he.

Introducing foreign experts has become very common in Guangdong Province. According to the figure reported by GD Foreign Expert Bureau, in recent five years, the number of foreign experts coming to work in Guangdong exceeds 130 thousand person-times per year, which accounts for one fifth in China, ranking the first place. The accumulated number of introduced overseas talents is 37 thousand, among whom 129 are Nobel Prize winners, academicians from developed countries, and lifelong professors and 19 are included in the national "Recruitment Program of Thousand Foreign Experts". How can we make full use of these "foreign brains" and make them better service the innovation- motivated development of Guangdong? According to Huang Xiangdong, the first thing to consider is the outer atmosphere. We must provide them with privileged conditions. He thinks that we do not lack of privileged conditions either in Guangdong or in Guangzhou.

"But there are also many enterprises in which talents cannot perform well because they are not trusted in many cases." According to Huang Xiangdong, who has introduced many foreign experts, in order to make good use of "foreign brains", we must show our trust to those real talents when they have come here. We should provide them with a platform and entrust them with important post to make them perform steadily and in a long run. "Now in many enterprises, talents always leave short after being introduced. What is the reason? There must be a problem of corporation culture and trust. They do not feel happy working there, or they are not entrusted to do practical tasks."

"In addition, for example, high-level experts often get paid by a salary system different from ordinary employees. "If all the employees don't like the introduced talent and think that he performs worse than them but gets better paid, that is also a problem." In Huang Xiangdong's opinion, optimizing allocation is an art and a technique. "The key is how the main management members of the company treat talents, and how they really trust and cherish talents."

"The talent has both strong points and weak points. He is strong on one hand and weak on the other hand. We must tolerate his weakness and exploit his strengths. If we only want to take some advantages of him but do not trust him, we definitely cannot make full use of his talent." says Huang Xiangdong.

Guangdong "Unmanned Aerial Vehicle" is Flying over Global Sky

The Legend of EHANG as Entering Dubai

The news was quickly spreading on the front page of many mainstream media and was called by many people as "Guangdong's Pride". Dubai local media Arabian Business, by quoting the statements of Dubai Office of Transportation, reported on 13th February that "EHANG 182" was equipped with touch panels in front of customers' seats. The drone would fly to the preset destination where customers had selected on the map. The flight was actually monitored and controlled by the ground control center. Dubai Civil Aviation Administration had issued the test flight license. The UAE Telecommunication was responsible to provide 4G network for the communication between the drone and the ground control center.

On 14th, the British Media BBC, by quoting the opinion of Doctor Steve Wright who was an aviation expert from University of West of England, reported that before it could fly carrying passengers, the drone must pass an unmanned flight test for over 1000 hours.

The unmanned aerial vehicles from Gaungdong are showing the honor and dream of "flying over global sky". Following DJI's occupation of global consumer drone market, industrial application technology is also set off. In addition to EHANG passenger-carrying drones, Guangzhou

Xaircraft Company is the first to set up affiliates in Japan, engaging in the domain of plant protection in Japan. Regardless of UAV toys, the overseas hot sales of drones can be deemed as an industrial success, an exportation of high value-added manufacturing industry.

In January 2016 in the U.S., "EHANG 184" was exhibited on the National Consumer Electronics Show for the first time. It was known as the first low altitude short-to-medium-distance automated passengercarrying aircraft. " 184" means 1 passenger, 8 propellers and 4 obtrusive arms. According to the introduction on EHANG official webpage, the 240 kg- net-weight " EHANG 184" is only electronically powered, which promises a 25-minute flight at sea level, with an average cruising speed of 60 km/h and a designed flying height up to 3500 meters over sea level. The drone's rated load is 100kg, with a trunk capable of holding an 18-inch luggage. Besides, " EHANG 184" is also equipped with an independent coding key to encrypt its

▲ Xiong Yifang, founder of EHANG

▲ EHANG passenger-carrying drone

communication systems.

According to public information, Guangzhou EHANG was established by Hu Huazhi and Xiong Yifang in 2014. In December of the same year, it received an A-class financing of 10 million dollars from GGV Capital, then a B-class financing of 42 million dollars in August 2015. Now the company has around 300 personnel.

One is model airplane enthusiast and technology enthusiast, one has overseas study experience, and one is good at marketing. In 2014, three business starters encountered in Guangzhou, and then a drone company named EHANG was born in Tianhe District. From then on, this drone company which represents Guangzhou is developing extraordinarily.

In 2014, coming back to China to start up a business after graduation from Duke University in America, Xiong Yifang met Hu Huazhi in Beijing who was demonstrating the unmanned aerial vehicle to the investor. That was the year when unmanned aerial vehicles were springing up. The leading drone company DJI which was located in Shenzhen acquired nearly 70% share of the global commercial drone market. More and more companies started to enter the domain of unmanned aerial vehicles, among which the internet enterprises especially MI and TENCENT were reported many times to expand their business to make drones. But in Guangzhou at that time there were no drone companies.

When Xiong Yifang later got to know the sales talent Yang Zhenquan, the three chimed in easily. They developed products aiming at the automatic drone market. People can easily control the flight of drone by simply installing an APP in their cellphone, and they can also make the drone follow them automatically.

EHANG, riding on the wind of drone industry, was developing rapidly like a rocket shooting to the sky. It got a financing of 10 million dollars only half year after its establishment. Its estimated value had increased by 25 times within 6 months. And the company was assessed by the American magazine *Fast Company* as one of the top 50 most innovative companies in 2014, ranking the second. According to Yang Zhenquan, Guangzhou is an internationalized trading metropolis and a place where the regulations and supply chains are very suitable for making hardware. They are very thankful to this hot land of innovation and business venture, which nurtures EHANG to grow at a "flying" speed.

On the Lantern Festival in 2017, Guangzhou witnessed the creation of a romantic Guinness record at Hai Xinsha—1000 drones teamed up to

▲ A thousand drones performing above the Pearl River.

make fancy performances, flying up to 100-meter height in the night sky scattering like thousands of dancing stars. They drew many excellent light paintings such as Golden Rooster Crowing, Welcoming New Year, and Beautiful Landscape of China, etc. A Guinness world record of "the largest UAV formation flight performance" was created. This "thousand drones changing" performance was provided by the Guangzhou Chi-Made Company of EHANG.

On the night of the Lantern Festival, when the clock hand pointed to 9, "Take off", at hearing the countdown voice from the interphone, 60 artists from Guangzhou Symphony Orchestra started to play the famous symphony *Yellow Riverthe Third Movement,* and 1000 intelligent aerial cameras GHOSTDRONE2 were rising slowly along with the music. In Huacheng Plaza which was on the opposite side of Haixinsha across the river, the crowded audience all raised their head staring at the most fantastic performance. Behind this performance, EHANG started to develop the drone formation performance technology two years ago. They decided to employ real-time communication network of UVA formation to ensure that the whole performance would not be affected even when single drone broke down or suffered from communication obstruction.

The most outstanding point of this Guinness record breaking was that only one person, one computer and one-key control were needed at the backstage. A technical person said that the UVA formation performance conducted at Guangzhou session of 2016 CCTV Spring Festival Party was actually controlled by many top players invited from around China by using remote controllers, in order to lower technical requirement and risk. Now in this performance there were 1000 drones. It was impossible to hire 1000 players to control them on site. Therefore, engineers designed a set of high efficient remote control system of UVA formation, which would

▲ The performance site of "City of Fireworks".

simultaneously tell every aircraft how to fly, where to stay, how to change team pattern, and what light color to put on, etc.

In 2017, the "Circles of Friends" all around the world were occupied by all kinds of UAV formation flight performances. At this year's CCTV Spring Festival Party, the unmanned aerial vehicle appeared again. One type of pocket drones finished a highly difficult indoor-stage big formation flight in the show "City of Fireworks", which made it become the face and ability representative for science at that party. International technology companies all treat the unmanned aerial vehicle as a powerful weapon for them to conquer the entertainment industry and to build up a good brand image.

From the Guangzhou Session of 2016 CCTV Spring Festival Party when UAV formation flight performance became popular overnight, eve of last Summer Davos Forum ceremony when 36 drones were dancing in front of Klaus Schwab, founder and Chairman of the World Economic Forum, to the current Guinness record, they all signify Guangzhou's desire for building an "intelligence made" city with technological factors. China is the market where the UAV industry is growing most vigorously, and Guangzhou becomes the brightest stage of unmanned aerial vehicles for the moment.

Wang Tao:
Unreasonably Enthusiastic
about the Sky

In addition to Guangzhou EHANG, there is another UAV giant in Guangdong—Shenzhen DJI, whose products occupy nearly 70% share of global civil small drone markets. DJI focuses on markets in European countries, from which nearly 80% of its total past sales is gained. The first mega millionaire of global UAV industry is a Chinese named Wang Tao. By Forbes's definition, Wang Tao is the owner of DJI.

Now DJI can sell several hundred thousand unmanned aerial vehicles—most are its main type—the Phantom series. From 2009 to 2014, the sales revenue of DJI has been increasing by two to three times per year. In May 2015, DJI got an investment of 75 million dollars from Accel Partners, while the personal assets of Wang Tao, who own 45% of the company share,

▲ Wang Tao, founder of DJI

would reach at nearly 4 billion dollars.

The whole globe is paying attention to this company. Unmanned aerial vehicles are being used for commercial purpose at a large scale: UAVs transmitted real-time aerial images for Golden Globe Award; Rescue workers drew maps of disaster-affected areas depending on UAVs during the earthquake of magnitude 7.8 in Nepal; Farmers in Iowa use UAVs to monitor their cornfields; Facebook will provide wireless internet connection in African farming areas by using self-own UAV products; DJI unmanned aerial vehicles also appear at the shooting sites of *Game of Thrones* and the latest *Star Wars*.

On Wang Tao' s office door there are two rows of Chinese characters—" Only bring your brain to work" and "Don't bring your emotions to work". The person in charge of DJI is following those rules. He is a leader whose languages are fierce but behaviors are quite rational.

▲ Unmanned aerial vehicles at film shooting sites.

▲ Phantom 4 Pro+ intelligent unmanned aerial cameras.

He works more than 80 hours a week, with a single bed beside his desk. Wang Tao was born in 1980. He got fascinated by the sky when

he was a primary school boy. He started to become full of imagination about the sky after he had read a comic book telling a story about a red helicopter's adventures. At the age of sixteen, he got a high score in an exam, and his parents rewarded him with a remote-control helicopter that he had dreamed of for a long time. But, he broke that complicated thing before long, and did not receive the parts used for replacement from Hong Kong until several months later.

Since his academic performance was not so outstanding, his dream of getting admitted to the first-class American universities did not come true.

At that time, his favorite universities were MIT and Stanford, but after being rejected, he had to take the second best. He finally went to Hong Kong University of Science and Technology, majoring in electronic engineering. In the first three year of undergraduate study, Wang Tao always failed to find a target for his life. But in the fourth year when he developed a set of helicopter flight control systems, his life was changed.

It may be said that Wang Tao had sacrificed everything for the last group project. He even skipped classes and stayed up late till 5 o'clock in the morning. Though the hovering function of the airborne computer that he developed went wrong one night before when it should be shown in class, his efforts were not in vain. Li Zexiang, Professor of robot technology at HKUST, discovered Wang Tao's leadership talent and his comprehension ability of technology.

So, under his recommendation, this persistent student continued his study as a postgraduate. "I am not very clear whether Wang Tao is smarter than others." said Li Zexiang, "But, those who get high scores may not have excellent performance at work." Li Zexiang was DJI's adviser and investor at its early stage, and now is the chairman of the company board, owning 10% share.

At first, Wang Tao made prototypes of flight controller in university dormitory. In 2006, he, together with two classmates, came to China's manufacturing center—Shenzhen. They worked in an apartment with three rooms. Wang Tao put all the rest of the scholarship he had won at university into the research and development. DJI sold to Chinese

▲ DIY Drones is the gathering center for drone amateurs.

universities and state-own power companies 6000 dollars of parts, which were welded on the holders of their DIY drones.

As the core team had been established, Wang Tao continued product development and started to sell his products to foreign amateurs, who sent him e-mails from countries such as Germany and New Zealand. In America, Andrew, Chief Editor of Wired magazine, created the message board DIY Drones for drone amateurs, some of whom proposed that drone design should be transformed from single-rotor to quad-rotor because quad-rotor was cheaper and easier to program. DJI started to develop more advanced flight controllers equipped with automatic driving function. When the development was finished, Wang Tao brought them to some small trade shows for promotion, such as the Wireless Remote- Control Helicopter Assembly held in Mansi City, State of Indiana, in 2011.

By late 2012, DJI had owned all factors required for making a complete drone: software, propeller, holder, gimbals and remote controller. Finally, in January 2013, the company issued "Phantom", the first quad-rotor aircraft which could take off at any time. It could fly within one hour after being unpacked, and it would not be dismantled at first falling. Thanks to its simplicity and usability, Phantom successfully broke into the non-professional drone market.

It is said that Wang Tao also needs to deal with all kinds of corporate spying. He asserted that the new drone companies emerging during last two years used to get DJI's designs illegally.

In recent years, DJI keeps expanding its overseas markets and has built up 70 offices step by step, stationing in all cities by light office mode. To be specific, there is sales and technical support in Japan, sales office in Korea, technical and logistics support in Germany and Holland, sales and marketing in Hollywood Northern America, research and development center in Palo Alto, and office in New York.

In overse as and even the whole global consumer markets of drones, DJI can be said to be of terminal dominance. From 2011 to 2015, its revenue was increasing by 3 to 5 times per year. According to statistics provided by DJI, its sales revenue in 2015 reached at 6 billion yuan. As the base was enlarged, the revenue growing speed slowed down in 2016, compared with that in 2015. The growth rate was around 60% to 70%.

▲ DJI flagship store in Seoul Korea.

Calculated by 65%, DJI's revenue of last year was around 9.9 billion yuan.

Now more than 80% of DJI's revenue is gained from overseas, Northern

America being the largest market followed by Europe. In 2016, the growth rate in Australia was relatively large.

The UAV:
Transfigured into a
Hard-working Farmer

Guangzhou XAIRCRAFT is another big name among the UAV brands in Guangdong. In XAIRCRAFT's eyes, the unmanned aerial vehicle is a hard-working farmer. She is entering the plant protection market in Japan, competing with Yamaha.

In November 2016, Yamaha's new UAV Fazer R was formally launched, at a sales price of 1.34244 million yen (that is 871.1 thousand yuan), equipped with a fuel injection engine of 20.6kW. Fazer R can spray pesticides to plants from the air, covering a farm area of nearly 4 hectares every time, and can carry 32 liter pesticides at most. In October of the same year, XAIRCRAFT also issued its latest P20 plant protection UVA and agricultural UVA flight control, and announced the launching of UAV sales and leasing business. It is known that the brand new P20 2017 plant protection UAV system includes drones, GNSS RTK positioning device (handheld mapping device, mobile base station, and fixed base station), A2 intelligent handheld terminator,

▲ Peng Bin, founder of XAIRCRAFT

pesticide box, injection machine, intelligent battery and charger. The system sells at 94999 yuan, while bare drone at 48500 yuan. And ordinary users can also choose to rent P20 plant protection UVAs by payment based on work volume.

XAIRCRAFT which was founded in 2007 has begun to develop plant protection UVA since 2012. It has made significant breakthroughs in agricultural UVA sector and has obtained many national and international technology patents. On 24th January, XAIRCRAFT announced the establishment of its Japanese affiliate and to formally stretch out the network of P20 plant protection UVA sales and plant protection service in Japan.

According to Peng Bin who is the founder of XAIRCRAFT, through years of development in China, XAIRCRAFT has gained certain capacity in both technology and manufacture of agricultural UVAs, which has even reached certain advanced level. They choose to enter Japanese market because Japanese agriculture is facing the same problems as Chinese agriculture does, which are aging population, sharp increase of labor cost, and decrease of farming population,

▲ XAIRCRAFT UVAs are entering Japanese agricultural production sector.

etc. But those problems occur in Japan much earlier than in China, which makes Japan be in stronger need of that kind of automatic agricultural UVAs.

As reported by the British *Financial Times*, few people outside Japan know that UVAs have been playing a very important role in Japanese farms since 1980s, when the motorcycle manufacturer Yamaha developed unmanned helicopters which were used to spray pesticides and to plant crops. On the dining-table of Japanese families, one in every two bowls of rice comes from the crops watered by Yamaha UVAs.

In the Chinese UVA sector, many companies choose to make multiple developments, while XAIRCRAFT chooses to focus on agriculture sector which is relatively less popular. Up to October 2016, Xplanet which is owned by XAIRCRAFT has established a service team of around 800 persons, covering a working area over 2 million hectares in 14 provinces around China and providing UVA plant protection services to nearly 100 thousand users. Besides, XAIRCRAFT has built up service headquarters in Xinjiang and He'nan.

"We have actually explored its applications in many sectors including logistics, public security, and the military, but in the process of final exploration we chose agriculture." Peng Bin says that agricultural market is broader, which can provide the companies like XAIRCRAFT with a better chance to exercise their abilities; secondly, there is much space in agriculture to be changed with technology, which is also the XAIRCRAFT's original target that we wish to use our products or technology to solve certain technical problems.

There are four basic processes in agriculture. During the whole agricultural production cycle, ploughing, planting, managing and harvesting are the four basic factors, of which XAIRCRAFT participates in the managing process.

"XAIRCRAFT services farmers through two channels: the first one is XAIRCRAFT's self-run team, who can provide the government or big farmers with the spraying service, which is only charged against surface, for example, 10 or 15 yuan per hectare without buying UVAs; the second one is that XAIRCRAFT has many partners who can provide services to local farms and growers." says Peng Bin, "As rural lands are becoming more and more centralized and land transfer is becoming faster and faster, more and more farms will need such kind of services. In the future, agriculture will be a sector with finer and finer division of labor."

▲ Plant protection UVA system

Guangdong College
Startup Elites

Chen Di: A Company Carefully Advanced Step by Step against Incessant Occurrences

Chen Di, a graduate of class 2006 majoring in computer at South China University of Technology (hereinafter referred to as SCUT), was listed in "China's Top 30 Entrepreneurs under 30 Years Old" in the Chinese version of Forbes, who made such a comment on those listed entrepreneurs: " These young people who have shown their innovative ability in technology, product, and commercial mode have already acquired very powerful startup spirit and revolutionary capability."

According to the teachers and students of the School of Computer Science and Engineering at SCUT, Chen Di was a "technology enthusiast" and a "contest enthusiast". "I don't like doing written assignments, but it doesn't mean that I don't like study." Chen Di' s passion for study was

▲ UMI's business system diagram

demonstrated not only by his enthusiasm for engaging in practices and experiments but also by his strong self-learning spirit. During the sophomore year, in order to join his senior schoolmate who had won a prize at the national challenge cup to develop a game, Chen Di, after finishing the classroom homework, stayed at the library to learn more computer technology knowledge until everyone had gone almost every day.

▲ Chen Di, founder of UMI

"SCUT's academic atmosphere was very free and open, and the school also encouraged us to do experiments. All those factors contributed a lot to my choice as to start up a business later on." Chen Di said, it was from the sophomore year that he started to participate in big contests such as "IBM Mainframe Application Innovation Contest", "Microsoft Elite Challenge", and "National Information Security Contest for College Students", etc. "The practical experiences with those famous enterprises in doing some practical training projects greatly contributed to my increasing hand-on ability." Chen Di is very grateful to his alma mater for providing him so many opportunities to exercise his knowledge. Those platforms not only taught him how to make project management and team cooperation but also guided him to try and to become sure about a suitable development direction. All that made a very good foundation for him to start up a business.

In fact, Chen Di who was born in Chaoshan had dreamed about becoming an entrepreneur since very young. Having participated in many contests and obtained some achievements, something called "innate commercial sensitivity" attacked his brain. He made repeated comparison and considerations, from big computers to PC markets. Based on his unconscious "commercial risk evaluation", he decided to start from mobile phone games.

"The young think it is a new market full of fun and chances." In the summer of 2007, Chen Di bought a cheap second-hand intelligent mobile phone from Zhonghua Plaza and started to program mobile applications with his classmates. When he realized how "cool" those mobile games could be, he organized a group of classmates who loved technology to form a workshop and started to make all kinds of mobile applications at the laboratory every day. Bluetooth Sanguo Kill, Bluetooth Doudizhu, 3D Table Tennis... were put on online for free download, and soon after, they were downloaded more than 2000 times per day. Before long, Chen Di's team was stuck in the dilemma of making charge or not. Faced with the inevitable conflict between developers and users, he said: "Some classmates enjoyed the pleasure of programming very much, but I prefered to transform technology into productivity. I would rather spend time to figure out how to commercialize a good product."

As a freshman, Chen Di made a website similar to Ctrip. But there were two problems: it was very hard and inefficient to sign contracts with

▲ The four co-founders of UMI from left to right: Cai Ruitao, Chen Di, Li Zhankeng, Ye Wensheng.

merchants; it was very difficult to develop business since the website visitor volume was too low. Considering his major—computer, he learned the first startup lesson: he must develop core technology competitiveness.

In the sophomore year, Chen Di started to study technology entrepreneurship, and had basically formed a start-up team. After finishing the IBM mainframe project, he also wanted to establish a national credit system. But looking back, it was very difficult for a young start-up team to commercialize that project which was awarded as an excellent application but was not commercialized. He also participated in some contests organized by Microsoft, in which he was mainly required to develop some games and applications based on Microsoft frameworks. During the

Olympic Games, Chen Di became an intern in Microsoft Beijing. He learned a lot there: "At that time I realized that PC startup era had gone."

In 2008, Chen Di's team participated in the National Information Security Contest for College Students held by Chengdu University of Electronic Science and Technology. They submitted a mobile application, the design principle of which was to record user's unlocking force so that other people could not open the phone even if they knew the code but typed it with a wrong force and tempo. The programming code was very simple and not long, but it was highly appraised and got awarded with the second prize. "It gave us a lot of confidence to start up a business aiming at mobile internet."

In 2010, the year of graduation, Chen Di was faced with three options: to pursuit postgraduate study as a recommended student, to participate in the exchange program in Singapore, or to start up a business on his own. The last one seemed to be the most "unreliable". His instructor wished him to grasp the opportunity of being recommended, and some team members were leaving to take internship in TENCENT. "Chen Di, you start up a business, we will stay with you; you pursuit your postgraduate study, we will still be with you!" When Chen Di was struggling with those options, two of his classmates who were also his core team members, Li Zhankeng and Zhang Nuanhui, firmly announced their " alliance determination" to him. Coincidently, many years later, that year is called by people as "the first year of mobile internet era".

On 1st April 2015, the fifth anniversary of UMI, Chen Di posted a speech video for celebrating the fifth anniversary of the advertising platform Youmi on its official website. Passionately he says that five years ago Youmi, the first mobile advertising platform in China, was covering more than 200 districts and countries around the world and having strategic cooperation relations with 1500 medium channels in the world.

舊 　　　　 過渡 　　　　 新

▲ The evolution of UMI Logo

Mihui platform is another important chess that UMI has placed in its socialized marketing chessboard, following the APP advertising business "Youmi+Adxmi". It is designed to be a marketing platform focusing on socialized media. Now Mihui has accumulated more than 1000 opinion leaders, has cooperated with more than 100 thousand WeChat industrial official accounts, and has attracted more than 100 million fans.

So far, UMI has already made arrangements at all flow entrances of mobile internet, has gathered strong resources from all directions, and has built up a marketing ecosphere of mobile internet. According to accessible information, UMI's revenue scale, net profit, APP coverage scale, and terminal coverage volume are all ranking top in the sector. UMI is certain about its advantages of development in the long-tailed market. It has

在创业路上，困难重重
只有你们，不离不弃
才能，乘风破浪
因为

创业不仅是一个人的梦想

▲ Cartoons of Chen Di's entrepreneurship on UMI website.

refused being acquired, insisting on developing independently, and determines to make the biggest independent mobile marketing platform in China.

In that year, UMI was selected as one of the 2015 Forbes China's Most Promising Unlisted Companies Top 10 and as 2015 China's Best Mobile Advertising Platform.

On 4th March 2016, UMI managed to get a financing of 250 million yuan at the New OTC (Over the Counter) Market, which renewed Chen Di's knowledge about the New OTC Market. He said that the whole financing process fully displayed the charm of the New OTC market. And the financing result was out of his expectation. The intended amount of funds was nearly 400 million, if at that time (when releasing the *Stock Issuance Plan*) we had not set the financing limit at 250 million or below, the financing amount might be bigger. Besides, the financing was very efficient that it only took one and a half months to get 250 million. The efficiency was increased a lot since we did not need to negotiate with VCs one by one.

As for future strategies, Chen Di describes a blueprint with "one horizontal line and several vertical lines": UMI takes the globalized mobile advertising platform as the "horizontal line" to expand its advertising business, and by taking advantages of the mobile advertising platform, it could focus on the "vertical lines" such as games, e-commercial, finance, education and O2O to deepen its business lines, gathering upstream and downstream of the sector and forming UMI's uniquely-own eco flow network. As for mobile advertising this " horizontal line" itself, Chen Di shows firm and strong confidence in the original intention of UMI's developing strategies: "At first our customers were mostly APP advertisers, now we have extended our business to over traditional brands promotion, websites promotion, and WeChat or market activities. Besides, developers have also made relevant extensions, from small APPs in the past, to now big APPs, and WeChat official accounts including 'we. Media' accounts, etc."

Wang Ruixu: a Post-90s CEO Who Made Proposals to the Premier

On the morning of 27th January 2015, in one meeting room at Zhongnanhai, Premier of the State Council, Li Keqiang was chairing a forum for the people of Science Education Culture and Health Care (SECH) and the grassroots representatives. Guided by the staff, Wang Ruixu, bringing a speech draft, a notebook and a pen with himself, arrived at one of the meeting rooms at Zhongnanhai. "Everyone's seat was arranged in advance, and there was a name list of speakers with speech order in front the seats."

Wang Ruixu said, he did not only noticed that he was the seventh to give a speech, but also that he was the only representative of Guangdong and also the youngest among the representatives participating in the forum. There were totally 10 persons, including himself, Yaoming, Chen Daoming, and Xu Ningsheng, etc.

"It was not until that moment that I completely understood the meeting

▲ Wang Ruixu, founder of JZM

content: Premier Li Keqiang would chair the forum and listen to the opinions and suggestions on the Government Work Report (Exposure Draft) from the SECH people and the grassroots representatives." said Wang Ruixu.

" Soon after we had been seated, the Premier walked into the meeting room, smiling and holding hands with every present representative." said Wang Ruixu. Though he had practiced the scene a thousand times in mind, he still felt very nervous when he was truly holding Premier's hands and introducing himself to him. His hands were

sweating during the whole process. "But I could still feel the Premier's affinity."

"When it was my turn, I had calmed down." Though he had prepared a speech draft, he finished his speech basically without turning to the draft. "It was mainly about proposals on college students' entrepreneurship by referring to my own experiences: I hoped the government to actually implement the supporting policies for college students' entrepreneurship and to create conditions for college entrepreneurs to realize their dreams."

"The Premier made an immediate response that college students are very important forces for promoting mass entrepreneurship and innovation. We must 'build up bridges and roads' and create conditions for them to realize their dreams and values." said Wang Ruixu.

Whereas on the evening of 6th Feburary, Wang Ruixu also forwarded a message titled as *Why Has Chen Daoming Been Invited by the Premier to Attend the Forum at Zhongnanhai* in his Circle of Friends, and left a message saying that "It was very happy to sit with Mr. Chen."

About 5 minutes after the CCTV News on the evening of 27th January, our customer service center received a call from one media requiring making an interview on us. In the next 20 minutes, we received interview appointment calls from a dozen media one after another." Ellen, who is working at Wang Ruixu's company in media promotion, says: "Nearly all media raised such a question to us: what makes Wang Ruixu the representative of post-90s entrepreneurs to participate in the Forum in Beijing?"

To that question, JZM start-up team gave a "powerful" response: he does not occupy the Circle of Friends, does not show his financing achievement in a high-profile manner, neither has he been reported on any gossips. Compared with those post-90s labels such as unscrupulousness, arrogance, and infantilism, people would prefer seeing other aspects of the post-90s, as being brave, persistent, practical and hard-working. And Wang Ruixu just happens to be a good example who insists on being the most hard-working and most persistent post-90s young entrepreneur."

Having participated in the Premier's Forum, Wang Ruixu became very popular. But his work was basically the same as usual, just as those things had never happened. On the morning of 29th January, he went to work as usual, and in the afternoon, he appeared in the 12th exchange meeting. He proposed suggestions on the establishment of one-stop service incubator base: "I hope that the incubator base can be made more of public welfare and of less commercial elements, and can provide one- stop supporting services including the service for college student's policy application."

Wang Ruixu has graduated from Guangzhou University of Chinese Medicine for only half a year. Guangzhou Joiway Technology Ltd that he founded in the third year of his undergraduate study has successfully received a second round of Angel Investment and an A-class financing of tens of millions. The company is valued more than a hundred million yuan. But few people know that the young CEO today used to be an internet addicted teenager, who performed very well in both study and business in university after he had turned over a new leaf. From internet addicted teenager, college student entrepreneur, to the Premier's guest, his growth process is an "inspirational novel".

Indeed, Wang Ruixu has an extraordinary "resume": in addition to the 5 scholarships he won during his study at Guangzhou University of

▲ The young start-up team of JZM.

Chinese Medicine, he also won more than 30 prizes including the titles of "China's Excellent Volunteer of Science Popularization" and "Thousand Volunteer" , the first prize of the first Guangzhou Creativity and Entrepreneurship Contest for the Youth, the golden prize of Guangdong Entrepreneurship Practice "2014 Challenge Cup", the first prize of the "Mobile Internet Design Contest of Guangdong, Hong Kong and Macau", Medicated Diet Contest of Guangzhou University of Chinese Medicine, etc. And he also won each of the national and provincial training projects for entrepreneurship and innovation. He is a typical young entrepreneur who does well in both study and business.

His start-up experience is much more extraordinary. He started up a business in mobile APP, while he was majoring in a totally different area, the discipline of "Resources and Development of Chinese Medicine". Before starting up a business, he used to work as security guard and to sell small goods on the street. He established the Modeng Team to make campus promotion for enterprises in the sophomore year. And in the third year, he founded the Joiway Technology with 70 thousand yuan he had saved, establishing a start-up team of 15 persons, which mainly focused on promoting "JZM" where college students could search for reliable parttime job information. He used to win the first "pot of gold" for starting up a business with a part-time job plan printed at 0.8 yuan.

It is out of imagination that Wang Ruixu used to be an "internet addicted teenager". Wang Ruixu was born in Shantou, at a family which ran a wool factory. He started to assist his parents in handling the factory account when he was 11 years old. Since junior high school, Wang Ruixu started to visit the internet bar frequently, almost staying there several hours every day. "Once in order to pass an online game, during the whole 7-day May Day Holliday, me and my younger brother, we stayed all day long in the internet bar, taking turns in playing the game for 12 hours each one, and we even could not spare a time for eating." recalled Wang Ruixu, before long, I became a definite problematic teenager who played online games, smoked, drunk, and skipped classes. It never rains but it pours. Before the senior high school entrance examination, his parents' factory was suddenly faced with crisis bearing a huge debt, and his family went bankrupt. Graduated from junior high school, Wang Ruixu handed to his mother an entrance examination sheet scoring 280. His mother slapped him heavily in the face. "My mother was crying. I could imagine how sad and helpless she was." Wang Ruixu was drawn back to the cruel reality, and he started to realize that he had to take on the heavy family responsibility.

So he proposed to take over his father's factory, which was however strongly against by his father. "He did not receive good education. So he did not want me to follow his old path." said Wang Ruixu.

Wang Ruixu was sent back to junior high school. His parents also ceased to let him study on his own, instead, they started to spend more time in monitoring his study. And in order to help him get rid of internet addiction, they intentionally sent him to a junior high school where there was no internet bar nearby.

Wang Ruixu got rid of internet addiction, studied very hard, got

admitted by Shantou Overseas
Chinese High School in the next
year, and then was admitted by
Guangzhou University of Chinese
Medicine through the college
entrance examination.

In the freshman year, he met
his girlfriend. In order to maintain
a relationship, he was always lack of
money. Every time when he called
for money, he could feel his

找兼职就用兼职猫，
喵了个咪！

www.jianzhimao.com

▲ JZM's advertising page is colorful and lively, which goes well with young people's taste.

mother's disappointment through the phone. His family was still in heavy
debt due to bankruptcy. "I was macho as a typical Chaoshan man. I
unconsciously wanted to protect my mother and did not want her to feel
sad for me again". Wang Ruixu made a big determination as to earn money
on his own. However, he, longing for a part-time job, was cheated by bad
agents out of much money.

Wang Ruixu started up a business at Guangzhou University of
Chinese Medicine. He worked on a 1.5m-long and 0.6m-wide table,
located in the east of the canteen, with a capacity of holding 4 persons. On
this table, Wang Ruixu recruited his team members one by one. They
formed the Modeng Team and worked hard for their business. "At that
time, even a smile from a senior female worker in the canteen was a great
encouragement for me."

From chagrin, discrimination, bitterness, persistence, and fighting, they gained the expansion of business, increasing number of team members from " song-and-dance duet" to "a choir of forty", and increase in revenue from zero to 150 thousand. It was also on that table that Wang Ruixu started to think about the future. Under the pressure of team development, and out of his unforgettable experience of college students part-time job market, Wang Ruixu founded the Joiway Technology Ltd and initiated the development of college students part-time job platform— the JZM. But at that time they had not enough money for the research and development. So except the technical, all the other team members engaged themselves again in campus agency and part-time jobs for a simplest purpose: to support the technical.

In 2013, he had owned a second table which was 2m in length and 0.8m in width, a phone, and a computer, and he worked with a group of like-minded young entrepreneurs.

It was located in a creative industry park in Baiyun District, a special free service area provided by Guangzhou Youth League for the youth to develop their business.

In the first Guangzhou Creativity and Entrepreneurship Contest for the Youth, the Youth League invited some experts and venture capitalists to "choose the horse". As an outstanding "dark horse",

Wang Ruixu was chosen. He did not only win the championship but also got a venture capital financing.

It was those painful experiences of being cheated when looking for part-time jobs that inspired Wang Ruixu to make "JZM". It was also because of that, he was very careful about the reliability of the posted information. In that contest, his "JZM" project did not only win the championship but also got a venture capital financing. Now, under Wang Ruixu's leadership, "JZM" has already attracted a million users and has successfully got a second round of Angel Investment and an A-class financing of ten millions. Faced with the problem of fierce internet "homogeneous competition", Wang Ruixu is very confident: "It will instead motivate our potentials to make this sector better."

He says that starting up a business is to make money, and as CEO, he has the responsibility to provide a better life to his team members. "So, starting up a business not making money is to behave like a hoodlum."

"As a grass-root post-90s from village, I cherish very much what I have now." Wang Ruixu uses his actions to bring new labels on the post90s: brave, persistent, practical, and hard-working. At the beginning, as CEO of the team, Wang Ruixu had to take full charge of all affairs such as promotion, operation, and public relation. "My work was allinclusive. I provided help anywhere I was needed. As the leader, I was obliged to provide guidance to others." Now, as the responsibility division is becoming clearer and clearer and the team is getting bigger and bigger, Wang Ruixu is mainly in charge of coordinating the whole company."

Wang Ruixu is working very hard, basically from 9 o'clock in the morning to 12 o'clock at night. "He seems able to do 10 persons' work and often helps to do other work." There was something wrong with his body when he was in Beijing, but on the next day Wang Ruixu insisted on going to work and attending the meeting at which he was invited. For that, his explanation is: "Now that I am an entrepreneur, I must learn to take on all the responsibilities brought by this identity. As for work, I am companied by my partners. I feel very good working hard together with them."

Wang Ruixu indicates that as for activities related to entrepreneurship, once invited, he will always participate in them under general conditions. The Forum held on 27th January has brought more attention to Wang Ruixu. But for him and his team, only "behaving in low-profile and working in high-profile" is the unswerving principle. He keeps reminding his colleagues: keep working hard, never be cocky, and make good products steadfastly.

Pu Shaotao:
Uremia Forced Me to
Start up a Business

In the middle of May 2015, the fund account of South China University of Technology received 200 thousand yuan. The teacher was shocked by the donator's name—Pu Shaotao, a student of Grade 2005 who was diagnosed as having uremia and managed to finish his study with strong persistence, under the help of the university and its students. Since the maintenance treatment of his disease is costly, where is the 200 thousand yuan from?

In 2005, Pu Shaotao, from a village in Shanxi Province, was enrolled in South China University of Technology to become an honorable national defense student. Full of expectations for the future, he was diagnosed as having uremia in the end of 2006. Pu Shaotao did not complain nor blame on anyone; instead he chose to face the disease bravely. At that time, no matter he chose to accept renal transplantation or dialysis treatment, the costly medical treatment charge is unbearable both for him and his family from a remote village. Pu Shaotao had always been taking part-time jobs to support his life at university. He even seldom went home in order to reduce transportation expense. During his treatment in hospital, Pu Shaotao was optimistic and confident. To cooperate with the treatment, he insisted on drinking only one mouthful of water every day. He totally received a dozen dialysis treatments, which made him shake with great pain every time. But he never complained about it. Upon hearing the news, the teachers and students of South China University of Technology gathered a donation of more than 30 thousand yuan by the next day after he was sent to hospital. Later on, they organized several donations, charity performances and charity sales activities: some students sold their works of fine arts, some students donated half-year income gained from being private tutor, and some students organized charity performances, some students made a special website for him to report on his health condition and to ask for help... and the university also raised a love fund to help him.

After one year of treatment, he was basically getting well. After leaving the hospital, Pu Shaota came back to the university which provided him with a single dormitory. He insisted on making treatments four times a day, half an hour a time. Every day, the first thing he did after getting up was to make a dialysis treatment on his own before going to school. When he came back to the dormitory at noon, he continued to make another dialysis treatment, a third after class in the afternoon, and a fourth before going to bed at night. It was also himself who

▲ Pu Shaotao

changed dressing for the wound, disinfected the room, and had injections and took pills on time.

The future looked dim, but Pu Shaotao never gave up. He always tried his best to do what he could. Due to his health condition, Pu Shaotao had to give up being a national defense student. Then he started to learn his favorite computer programming on his own. "I have to learn a professional skill." Pu Shaotao started to think for himself. So he took computer as a selective course, and also learned it from online courses.

If someone was passing Pu Shaotao's dormitory at that time, he would see him making treatment and typing the keyboard at the same time. "Time seemed to pass very fast when I was learning programming." said Pu Shaotao with a smile on his face, learning had also transferred his attention from the treatment pressure.

On one occasion, hearing the teacher say that he wanted the national student website be revised, Pu Shaotao recommended himself to take the job without a second thought. Now it only takes him one week to make a website. But it took him one month at that time since he was not skillful enough. "I summoned up courage and handed in the work", while the teacher thought that the new website was pretty good. Knowing that Pu Shaotao was able to design websites, teachers, with great passion, introduced new "clients" to him. During his study at university, Pu Shaotao designed websites for a dozen schools, and also got some orders outside school. The "part-time job" earned him some money to support his life, but more importantly, it gave him more confidence.

In 2007, Pu Shaotao was elected as the "Self-improvement Star of Chinese College Students" with a majority of votes.

In spite of the great honor he had gained, he was still faced with huge survival crisis. What Pu Shaotao expected for the future was to find a job to support himself. He never thought of starting up a business until he was faced with the embarrassment of "unemployment upon graduation".

In 2009, as a consequence of the finance crisis, graduates were faced with an unprecedentedly difficult job-hunting season. Nevertheless, quite a few good software development jobs were offered to Pu Shaotao because of his strong programming technique. Should I conceal the truth? Pu Shaotao struggled in mind, but he finally decided to tell the truth.

One company called him to register. He told them about his disease and assured them again and again that the disease would not affect his working performance and his health condition would not have anything to do with the company. But he was still rejected. "I understood the company." said Pu Shaotao with a sigh, "But I still felt quite disappointed when I heard other students talking about the jobs they had found." Till then, Pu Shaotao totally gave up hunting for a job.

Most people start up a business out of interest or for pursuing a dream, but Pu Shaotao chose to start up a business because he found no other way out. Just at that moment, the teacher delivered a piece of good news to him: the government was encouraging graduates to start their own business and the qualified graduates could get an initial fund. Therefore, Pu Shaota got 100 thousand yuan to start his business.

After graduation, in a rented house he shared with others, Pu Shaotao alone started the business of website design and maintenance. He was struggling in hesitation as whether he should make recruitment or not since he was short of money. "What if I cannot get orders to support my personnel?" But one can never succeed if he never takes the first step. At last, Pu Shaotao cut off all the means of retreat and recruited 4 employees. They moved into another house with a surface of 140 m. Bearing great pressure, he had to do many things in person, and his body suffered a lot. One night at 10 o'clock, he delivered panels to his client. Then he missed the last bus for going home. It was raining hard that night. He walked for half an hour, which resulted in leg cramp. "I often stayed up late at night for orders only worth a few hundred yuan." Pu Shaotao was working extremely hard because he had no way to retreat.

More than one year later, Pu Shaotao realized that he did not make any money after deducting employee's salary and other expenses. In 2011, at his elder brother's advice, he turned to e-commerce, and became the first merchant who engaged in online make-to-order and sales of building materials and household products at TMALL. For business development, he moved from Guangzhou to Qingyuan. He registered and founded Qingxin Leyou Household Product Co., Ltd., of which the warehouse has been expanded from around 200 m to more than 1000 m. The company has developed into a specialized window track supplier.

There are more and more online stores of similar types, and price wars against them resulted in low profit. It is not good for the company's development in the long run. Pu Shaotao has made breakthroughs from marketing mode and service quality, wishing to be "the one and only". He has established an offline service network around China in more than 1000 cities. "From the first installer, Guangzhou, we founded others in Xinjiang and Tibet in half a year. Once you have placed an order, an installer would immediately go to your house to provide professional installation service."

Pu Shaotao has also developed an ERP system which is specialized in the management of customization orders. Earlier, by using the ordinary online store sales system, they had to make pricing adjustments manually by referring to a table every time when the client made one change. It was inefficient and error-prone. Now with the modified system, their work load is largely reduced: "The work that required 15 sales persons to finish now only requires 10 persons."

In order to provide clients with better services, the company proposed a " 20-yuan Rule " , i.e. if the client finds the product unsatisfactory (color difference for example), he will be compensated from several yuan to 20 yuan by the company. As a result, some clients may get a compensation of 20 yuan even if they have just bought a 10-yuan product.

High-quality products and good customer experience made Pu Shaotao's "Zhishang Household" flagship store become the first brand of curtain accessories at TMALL. Since 2012, "Zhishang Household" has been ranked as KA Merchant at TMALL. Products can be replicated, and services can be imitated. If a company looks for a long-term development and transformation, it is critical for it to hold the core technology. Now Pu

Shaotao is turning to intelligent household products. He is trying to realize a mobile control of all electronic household products. Now the hardware equipment is being tested. He says: "If it works, the customer will be able to open the air conditioner and fill up the bathtub before he arrives at home. In his words, "it is like installing a brain in the current product."

When the company is on track, Pu Shaotao repays the society in a more practical way. In Qingyuan, which is located in Northern Guangdong Province, most of his employees are not very well educated, who are mostly only graduated from senior high school, but they can get paid with four or five thousand yuan per month on average, some who are hard-working may event get more than ten thousand yuan. "It is even not difficult for them to buy a house." The company arranges health examinations for employees and also provides bonus to reward the excellent employees. Besides, he will donate 1 ‰ of every online order amount to the children in impoverished mountainous areas to help them go to school. Pu Shao also wants to open online sales channels for the agricultural products from Shanxi villages, wishing farmers to earn more money.

When he had finally saved some money, Pu Shaotao silently transferred 200 thousand yuan to the fund account of South China University of Technology, wishing to help students with serious diseases. He says: "At my most difficult time, it was the university and the society who gave me great love and help. Now that I have gained some power, I want to pass on that love and help."

When Factories and Villages Encounter the Internet

Factories are Revitalized by Internet+! Culture+!

Upon hearing the broadcasting in factory, workers were going home from work. Some of them were riding a bicycle taking his wife with him to buy food at the market located in the factory. Some of them, holding a ceramic teacup in hand and wearing the factory uniform and white gloves, were getting ready to take their children home from the school located in the factory. That is the memory of the workers who worked in the old factory located in Guangzhou Industrial Revenue in the 80s of the 20th century.

The Wechat headquarter located in the internet+ textile machinery plant

The TIT Creative Industry Center where Wechat headquarter is located and which is very well-known in South China grows out of the former Guangzhou Textile Machinery Plant founded in 1956 which was the largest textile machinery plant in South China at that time.

Today, the transformed TIT Creative Industry Center shows both a sense of old factory's vicissitudes and a cold-fashion sense of modern architecture. Extending from the front entrance towards the inner Center, there are 10 rectangular panel walls lined from cold color tone to warm color tone, the middle parts of which are hollowed with mannequin poses of different characters. In the Center, there are 21 primitive industrial factory buildings, crisscrossed pipe networks, and peculiar sculptures and industrial machinery models, scattering among more than 300 towering trees. Thus a peculiarly unique office space is woven. On the red brick factory walls are printed frescoes and slogans of strong historical characteristics saying "Cultivate the labor, Labor the cultivated". Those old industrial prints bring people back to 30 years ago.

There are around a dozen textile companies in the Center. Other companies are of sectors including internet technology, entertainment and media, architecture design, and catering, etc. Among them, the most famous is TENCENT WeChat headquarter which moved in two years ago and now occupies more than 5 factory buildings.

Employees are having meetings in twos and threes in the cafe near the company, and programmers are crazily clicking the keyboard in front of the computer...such scenes are not rare at TIT. By contrast, clothing shops are much less crowed. Most of them are playing high-end roles, self-positioning as "top" "customized" high-class clothing clubs, and selling clothes of approximately 800 to 2000 yuan.

▲ The beautiful door decorations, traditional walls, and modern clothes in TIT Center bring out the best in each other.

Turning off from the Center, we enter the E-commerce Industrial Zone, where the historic memory of this city is hovering and where the magnificent second entrepreneurship history raises the curtain.

Haizhu District which is located at the south of Guangzhou' s new central axis becomes the main "internet+" battle field, with an "e-commerce avenue of Guangzhou southern central axis" formed along the axis. Guang Yi International E-Commerce Industrial Park grows out of the former Guangzhou Diyi Pump Plant. The Park covers 38 thousand m2 and is mainly built for holding excellent big enterprises' headquarters and for incubating excellent breeding enterprises. It is included in e-commerce relevant supporting preferential policies of Haizhu District, and is positioned as a national-class e-commerce pilot park of cultural and technological integration. Now there are 45 enterprises in residence and 19 enterprises under incubation.

Having grown out of such transformation mode, the Park not only preserves the "Guang Yi" brand and style but also becomes a trademark of the "suppress the second industry and develop the third industry" project of Haizhu District.

The rapidly developing Guang Yi E-Commerce Park is ambitious, planning to transform and build up creative office buildings covering 30000-50000m, to introduce 3-5 famous e-commerce pilot enterprises, to gather 100 medium and small e-commerce companies, to realize an annual productivity density of 100 thousand yuan/m, tax density of 5000 yuan/m or above, total annual production value of enterprises in residence of more

▲ Bronze sculptures are made at TIT Creative Industry Center to revive the workshop scenes of the old days.

than 1 billion yuan, paying tax more than 150 million yuan, in three years. The operator "group of five industries" includes e-commerce, technology, creative industry park development, and professional institution of operation. The relevant responsible person, Zhang Minxu says that in the process of upgrading the factory zone into an e-commerce zone, physical space is only a foundation, which provides headquarter and breeding enterprises with "catalysts" such as administrative support, startup investment, industrial cooperation, and entrepreneurship atmosphere, and what is more important is to create the "chemical space" which makes enterprises succeed easily.

"For example, why would a company choose to place its office at the Park instead of in the office buildings at Tianhe North or Zhujiang New Town? The rent would be one factor, but employee's working status, creative space, and innovative communities are more important."

According to Zhang Minxu, the transformation of old factory into new e-commerce zone must be deeply rooted in the two big soils of local economic upgrades and urban upgrades, virtually realizing a transformation from "physical space" to "chemical space".

Culture+Museum is leading, and People's Printing House is designing the most advanced product

At the same time when the "suppress the second industry and develop the third industry" strategy is sweeping over Guangzhou, the creative industry is growing up. Old factory zones are being upgraded.

As "an art and living center defined by international standard", Redtory Art & Design Factory still preserves a strong factory style. Now, here we find galleries well-known both at home and abroad, design workshops, art display spaces, fashion shops, special restaurants and cafes. You can also feel young and fresh atmosphere brought by leisure art and entertainment. The young people who love culture and arts write passionately: "When you are alone, you will fall in love with this place."

In 1956, China's biggest can factory "Guangdong Can Plant" was born here. In 1994, it was renamed as " Guangzhou Ying Jing Qian Enterprise Group Company". As part of the "suppress the second industry and develop the third industry" project, "YIQ" moved out, and artists transformed the abandoned workshops into LOFT-style blocks.

Block-printed ancient paintings, bronze-type printed models, inkprinting equipment, salt-water -powered flashlight...the Guangzhou People's Printing House located in Yanzigang South Road is one of our memories along the Industrial Avenue. The printing production has been moved out from Haizhu District, while the old plant's brand stays. The factory has been quietly transformed into a "creative industrial park of packaging and printing culture", where we can find Guangzhou Printing Museum which

▲ The main entrance of Guang Yin Creative Industrial Park.

tells us about the printing history, the Research and Development Center of Anti-forgery Technology, and the Research and Development Base of Industrial Packaging Design.

The 60-year old Guangzhou People's Printing House is quite familiar to many Guangzhou residents. The food coupons, oil coupons, bond coupons, tax coupons, and residence booklets were all printed there. Since a few years ago, the Printing House has already started to make transformation quietly. The main printing production has been moved out to Baiyun District, while the old factory in Haizhu has become the first creative industrial park of printing culture in Guangdong Province.

Walking into the Creative Industrial Park of Printing Culture, we are mostly attracted by the Printing History Museum. The 800-square meter museum, which used to be a warehouse for printing inks and papers, now displays the whole printing history in epitome from oracle bone inscriptions to the latest digital printing. There we can see not only many entities of block printing and type printing but also the live performance of engraving Buddhist scriptures printing which was the most popular in Tang Dynasty.

There are also many very old printing machines being exhibited, which are, according the Printing House's responsible person, left by the old printing house. Among them we find the ink printing equipment with which the older-generation people are familiar — letters were carved on a stencil paper, which was then brushed by a brush full of ink, which then printed the letters on papers. Those who were studying at primary school in 70s or 80s all have all done exam papers printed in that way. Now the Museum is applying for becoming an education base of patriotism and popular science.

On the second floor are exhibited the entities representing the latest modern industrial design concepts. One of the exhibited items is very interesting. With an injection of 300ml light salt water, the flashlight can work for 100 hours. "You can even inject sea water or urine. It is the first choice at emergency." The designer is displaying and introducing this patented salt-water flashlight at the same time. Once launched, it attracted a lot of orders from Japan and became a necessity of Japanese earthquake emergency kits.

Near to the Industrial Center of Packaging Design is situated the Research and Development Center of Anti-forgery Technology, which has developed a dozen anti-forgery technologies that have been applied in

▲ Factory buildings in the Dong Fang Hong Creative Industry Park are transformed into modern offices.

packaging designs. The worldwide famous HP Company has also established an exhibition center in the Creative Industrial Park.

The transformation of the Creative Industrial Park where the Printing Museum is located will be divided into three phases, covering 10800 m with a total investment of 150 million yuan. In addition to the Printing Museum, there will also be High-tech R&D Area, Cultural Creation Design Area, Patented Technology Incubation Area, and Anti-forgery Technology Application Center, gathering a bunch of printing-related high-tech research and development companies, cultural creation companies, and packaging design companies.

The" factory museum" of old memories records the entrepreneurship history of Guangzhou

The rising of e-commerce centers and creative industry parks does not erase the glorious industrial development history of Guangzhou.

The 75-year old worker Mr. Huang often takes a walk in the Creative Park. He started to work in Guangzhou Textile Machinery Plant in 1968, when the factory buildings were surrounded by bamboos and seemed very deserted. "Its best time was in the middle of the 90s, when there were more than 1300 workers, one general manager and nine deputy managers, who were called as "top 10 generals" by many workers for fun."

More than half a century passing by, the heroes have turned from "plant generals" into creative talents. Mr. Huang is very satisfied: "I have not expected that most of the factory buildings are preserved after the plant was shut down. The factory building that was used by the supply department in which I was working now has become a hotel."

Xiaoshang, a college student who is preparing for the IELTS examination at a continuation school nearby, is showing TIT to his friends who are from Beijing. His introduction is very simple but powerful: "This is Guangzhou's version of 798 (a very famous creative park in Beijing)." At the north of the Creative Park, the construction of TIT Phase II is in full swing.

No. 313 Industry Avenue Middle, the three huge characters "Dong fanghong" written on the entrance door make people feel they were back to earlier ages. Dongfanghong Printing House was built in 1968. Since the 90s of 20th century, new printing houses were blooming. DFH was regarded as "the Whampoa Military Academy" in the printing sector, attracting many people to come to be apprentice. Later the House declined, and many private printing plants head hunted their technical personnel, who could easily pass the job interview without taking any examination as long as they were wearing DFH's uniform.

In 2009, DFH shut down the printing workshop and moved out from Guangzhou. Now "Dongfanghong" on the arched door is still shining but has become the brand of "Dongfanghong Creative Industry Park". The old factories are completely preserved with all kinds of slogans left on the brick walls. Now this area has already been occupied by photography studios, internet companies, and a "Research Institute of Brand Problems" which confuses most people...the old factory buildings are changed. There are no workers any more, but are the tourists who are attracted by its fame and models wearing peculiar clothes.

The glorious industry development history of Guangzhou arouses every visitor's feelings. The Xie Tong He Machine Plant, which was located on the west of White Goose Lake and by the side of Ming Ling Ancient Bridge, was fabulously well-known in Chinese history. In 1915, the first Chinese diesel engine was made there, which lifted a flag for Chinese modern national industry. After People's Republic of China was founded, it became part of Guangzhou Diesel Engine Plant. In 2011, that 100-year old factory was shut down and became a "Diesel Engine Museum", which displayed the historical working scenes of sweating workers taking the old machines as stage background.

Along with the development of industry and updates of technology, old production tools and materials are being constantly abandoned, those of which have been preserved contribute to today's "factory museum".

"Taobao" Shops are Flourishing at the Villages of Guangdong

Approaching 12 o'clock at night, it seems very quiet at Junpu Village, Jieyang City, Guangdong Province. Along the famous Intelligent Street of the village, most online wholesales shops have been closed. Peeping through the doors, you may see the packed clothes which are piled as a small mountain in some shops. As one of the most famous "Taobao" villages of Guangdong Province, Junpu village gained an online sales amount over 80 million yuan during the online shopping carnival " Double Elevens" in 2006. The success of Jupu Village's e-commerce is a good example for building the Junpu commercial zone in the east of Guangdong Province. Its experiences of development are being widely copied by other villages and towns in Jieyang.

Orientation training assembly of village-level service station of

▲ Guangzhou Conghua E-commerce Industry Park and Alibaba District-level Service Center of "Rural Taobao".

"rural Taobao" held at Wuhua County of Jiedong District, covering only 0.53 square kilometers, with 490 households of more than 2800 villagers. There are more than 350 households of nearly 2000 villagers engaging in online sales activities, opening more than 3000 online shops of all types and more than 320 real online wholesales shops. Here, except kids and the aged, all villagers are doing e-commerce. Many housewives also start to open online shops after receiving the free e-commerce training offered by the government. Now few people know that Junpu Village used to be a "problematic village" suffering from severe social conflicts. Changes have been made since three years ago, when several young workers came back from Guangzhou and started their online shop business on Taobao. They were then followed by countless villagers. Then Junpu Village, as becoming more and more crowed and more and more famous, was certified by the e-commerce giant Alibaba as one of the 14 "Tabao Villages" around china.

Now the big Junpu e-commerce zone has been basically established. The Junpu e-commerce mode, as a replicable experience, has been promoted by Jieyang government to all the villages in this city.

Yes! Village, this word has never been so close to the internet! On 15th February 2017, China's Ministry

▲ Junpu Village is located at Xichang Town in the east.

of Commerce issued a report on the establishment status of national agricultural product market system: the turnover of China's agricultural product e-commerce is expected to reach over 220 billion yuan in 2016. It is a fertile new land for the "villagers" of Guangdong. At the ends of the hot "agricultural e-commerce" network, more and more rural small shops are becoming village-level service stations for e-commerce enterprises, playing an important role of sending, receiving, and transmitting express packages.

"I have to handle at least a dozen packages per day." Zhou Tingting who is the shop owner of a village-level service station at the Taiping Town of Shixing County of Shaoguang City of Guangdong which is jointed to that network tells the media happily. She says, now the online shopping packages are mainly household appliances, clothes and daily necessities, which can be delivered by electronic tricycle. The logistics pressure is not great, and she can earn a commission of two to three thousand yuan per month.

In 2006, Guangdong set a target that by 2020, the rural e-commerce application level around the whole province is obviously increased, the supporting service system of rural e-commerce is basically established, the double-flow channel of urban and rural products is basically formed, the scale of agricultural products online sales and rural online shopping continues to expand, and the whole development level ranks top in the whole China. There will be 50 county-level e-commerce industrial parks and 100 town-level e-commerce operational centers built up around the whole province, realizing a full coverage of rural e-commerce service station in all administrative villages. Relying on e-commerce, information technology, and logistics network, based on the

▲ Crippled Zhou Tingting at the village Tabao service station.

"project of hundreds of thousands of rural markets", we should speed up the establishment of modern circulation network in rural area, and strengthen the service network, facility construction, and their connection of systematic logistics such as trading, sales and supply, and postal service, in order to facilitate the distribution of daily necessities to villages.

The college students, who are from rural areas and are admitted by urban colleges, are also trying their best to get villagers involved in sharing the internet bonus. Yuan Senlin, a rural student of Jinan University, heard a small story when he was conducting research in Xingning Meizhou during the sophomore summer holidays: a son who was working in Donguang sent some rice dumplings that were distributed by his company to his old father by express, but since the logistics service in rural area was under development and his father was not used to receive mails, that "fast delivery" became a "slow delivery", and the rice dumplings that were full of the son's love had become decay and uneatable when they were finally passed to the father's hands.

Yuan Senlin and other four "post-90s" who grew up in the same village and were studying in the city formed a team to start a project to build up a "rural-urban circulation" platform. The five young people were concerned about the same problem that since rural logistics and e-commerce were under development, it was difficult to deliver rural products to urban areas, and vice versa. The team he led hoped to build up a physical link to couple rural people and urban people by providing e-commerce services to farmers. Combining the research result and what they had learned, they divided the "rural-urban circulation" services into two sections, i.e., rural-urban logistics agency and online purchasing agency: as for logistics, they planned to set up warehouse headquarters in counties as gathering points of packages and to cooperate with convenience

▲ The group photo of "rural-urban circulation" team members.

stores which would act as distribution stations from which customers get the package on their own; as for purchasing agency, they had developed shopping guide platforms to help farmers to make "online shopping".

This small team started to prepare for the "Challenge Cup" National Contest of College Students Entrepreneurship which would be held in New Year. In two years' time, from project to participation, the "rural-urban" team had traveled through more than 20 villages and towns in Guangdong Province to conduct research. In one village of Shanwei City, the students met an old man whose daughter was out to work all year round. He had planted longan trees in the field. But since the purchasing price was low and he was too old, most of the longans were left on the trees and became decay. Upon the old man's consent, the team led by Yuan Senlin picked 100 kg longans and brought them back to Shenzhen to sell online. The 100 kg fresh longans were quickly sold out in 50 minutes.

"The 'longan' sales event represented a problem that Chinese rural areas were commonly faced with: it was hard to deliver high-quality agricultural products to urban areas. It did not only affect farmers' income but would also result in resource waste. The 'rural-urban circulation' plan was to solve the problem of 'exportation' and 'delivery'." Then, the express industry which played the central role in transmission became the focus of the "rural-urban circulation" team's research program...

Thus, the "rural-urban circulation" model was being modified again and again based on their careful researches. When they were participating in the contest in Wuhan, one judge made a comment excitedly after hearing their speech. They were finally awarded the national golden prize of the contest.

Of course, there are many other people who are optimistic about the future of Guangdong rural e-commerce. "The rural e-commerce is a very promising." Chen Haiquan, Dean of Guangdong Research Institute of Asia-Pacific E-commerce, makes such comment in front of the media. He says, Guangdong rural e-commerce turnover is conservatively estimated to reach 28 billion in 2017, 43 billion by 2020. There are many special agricultural products in Guangdong. Special agriculture-related industries covering flowers and plants, fruits, sea food, and meat have been established in about 85% of the counties around the whole province. And Guangdong is not only a place which produce a large quantity of agricultural products but also an important consuming and gathering place for the agricultural products coming from places outside Guangdong Province.

The Internet
Dreams of Urban Villages

On 23rd September 2016, Chinese Youth's Entrepreneurship and Employment Foundation signed a strategic cooperation framework agreement with Tianhe District Government of Guangzhou to build Chinese youth' s entrepreneurship communities varying from 5000 to 30000 square meters in each of the 21 sub-districts of Tianhe District. It also means that the first Chinese youth's entrepreneurship community "5ipark" in the province will be located in the Tianhe District of Guangzhou.

The youth' s internet entrepreneurship community "5ipark" is an internet incubation brand which is established by Wuxing Incubator Group, IDG Capital, and Chinese Youth's Entrepreneurship and Employment Foundation. There are plenty of reasons for her sturdy choice of locating in Guangdong.

Chen Zongxiong, Secretary of Chinese Youth' s Entrepreneurship and Employment Foundation of the Central Committee of the Communist Youth League, is ambitious: "This is the first cooperative project of Chinese youth's entrepreneurship community made by the district administrative. I hope it can become a national example of district administrative cooperation in Tianhe and can be replicated and promoted." He says, Chinese youth's entrepreneurship community will become an integrated base for entrepreneurship contests, entrepreneurship training, entrepreneurship services, entrepreneurship finance, entrepreneurship social communication, entrepreneurship promotion, and entrepreneurship credit investigation, acting as a start-up "micro city" of working, living, and entertaining for young entrepreneurs. Guangdong Province is chosen as its first location and Tianhe District as its first station because Tianhe District has pioneering advantages in the IT and internet industry in China. At the same time, the Tianhe District Government has always been working on the construction of incubators in urban villages and plans to transform about 4 million murban real estates into public entrepreneurship space.

According to the agreement, both parties jointly promote and implement the project of "Chinese youth's entrepreneurship community and the sub-brand 5ipark youth's internet entrepreneurship community", initiating and creating a model developing mode as "one sub-district one community", i.e., trying to establish youth's entrepreneurship communities varying from 5000 to 30000 square meters in every sub-district, so as to form a service system of youth's double entrepreneurship incubation and to establish a talent base of youth's innovation and entrepreneurship, which can provide integrated resources for incubation and generate scale effects by making the start-up enterprises of different sub-districts be uniquely particular and complementary to each other.

In addition, in every youth's entrepreneurship community there will be a public space which will provide the young entrepreneurs with free stations and basic incubation services. They will try their best to realize

3000 free stations in Tianhe District in 2 years. Both parties will also found the Tianhe Sub-foundation of Chinese Youth's Entrepreneurship Foundation to provide special investment for the projects and teams that choose to locate in the youth's entrepreneurship community.

The 5ipark youth's entrepreneurship community is a model built in Tianhe District, which will be a comprehensive incubator covering 5i innovation factories, 5i incubators, 5i accelerators, 5i entrepreneurship apartments, and 5i creation streets." Zhang Minxu, co-founder of 5ipark Youth's Internet Entrepreneurship Community, said, 5ipark would create a multidimensional community cultural system of variant community combinations, diversified urban new spaces, regional or industrial activities of great influence power, specialized enrollment evaluations and community member services, and transplantations of trans-regional or trans-industrial resources. "It is not only to build up a fresh and new community space, but what is more important is to work with the enterprises and people in residence to form a more advanced urban working and living mode." explained Zhang Minxu, "5 ipark community is a prevailing public entrepreneurship space, an iterative product of startup space, and an innovative incubator."

In the cities located in southern Guangdong, urban villages are inspired with stronger and stronger new entrepreneurship dreams. The Tangxia Street located in Zhongshan Avenue West of Guangzhou is a typical street of urban villages. An area of 7.42 square kilometers is shared by two urban villages, Tangxia and Tangdong, where live 350 thousand residents, among whom 260 thousand are migrant workers. The number of migrant workers in those two villages is so huge that it can rank top among that of all urban villages in Tianhe District. And they produce 230 tons of rubbish per day, which is one-sixth of the total rubbish produced in Tianhe District. Similar to most of the urban villages in Guangzhou, Tangixa Street's roads are narrow, rugged, covered with scattering rubbish at every corner, and crossed by numerous electric wires.

In order to make sure that incubators can also be located here, the Street dismantled many escalators and iron stands that are blocking the roads, expanded and newly built asphalt roads nearly 3500 meters, built up pavements 3000 meters, installed traffic bars 4200 meters, unblocked and newly built 150 sewers, and fixed 26 flood points. After that, the "micro recycling" management mode was introduced: four closed-off managed auto roads enabled an orderly circulation of automobiles in the village, 500 HD cameras were installed...the orderly construction helped to increase the rent of local real estates by 30% and attracted a bunch of high-tech enterprises which had great market potentials and strong innovative abilities to become residents there. In 3 months' time, Tangxia Street concentrated on renovating the surrounding environment of the village company's real estates, and then a New OTC Market incubator of certain scale was established in its old factory area.

The construction of "public entrepreneurship space in urban villages" is still an ongoing event in Tianhe. One third of the 11-milion-m2collective real estates of urban villages will be transformed into cost-efficient and novel—designed innovative development space. The innovative fusion of urban villages is taking effects. Tianhe District is opening its arms to numerous innovators and entrepreneurs by using relatively low cost and with comprehensive new service chains of innovation and entrepreneurship. At the same time, the urban villagers in Tianhe, who used to make a living by leasing their real estates, are jointing in the new economic trend. Some village collective economic organizations are even involved in investing in the internet ecologic home project, becoming part of the global innovation chain.

一隻改變世界的企鵝

馬化騰的三次危機

一九八七年九月，德國教授措恩在北京出席一個科技研討會。經過一番調試後，他將北京的計算機應用技術研究所和卡爾斯魯厄大學計算機中心實現了計算機聯結。

九月十四日，措恩與中國的王運豐教授共同起草了一封電子郵件，寫道：「Across the Great Wall we can reach every corner in the world.」（越過長城，我們可以到達世界的每一個角落。）「This is the First Electronic Mail from China to Germany.」（這是第一封中國到德國的電子郵件。）內容和標題均由英、德雙語寫成，也就是後來知名的「越過長城，走向世界」的郵件。在該郵件上署名的除了王運豐、措恩教授，還有十一個中德雙方的參與工作的人員。

但 CSNET 郵件服務器上卻存在著一個問題——PMDF 協議中一個漏洞導致了死循環，導致這個郵件的成功發出被延遲。經過諮詢並得到了 CSNET 信息中心的確認：這個問題一直存在，尤其是在電話線路不好的時候。措恩教授的助手邁克爾·芬肯(Michael Finken）在北京與留守卡爾斯魯厄的格德·威克(Gerd Wacker）共同努力，克服工作時差等多方障礙，用軟件彌補了線路不穩造成的信號混亂。九月二十日，這封郵件終於穿越了半個地球到達德國。

到了今天，四十五歲的廣東汕頭人馬化騰創辦騰訊整整十八年了。剛剛過去幾個月的二〇一六年十一月十一日，是騰訊十八週年紀念日，當天馬化騰聯合總裁辦成員給在職員工、離職員工、外包人員和公司服務人員發出了總計三千萬元的微信紅包。

這並不是高潮。因為馬化騰晚些時候還宣布了一個決定，給在職員工每人三百股騰訊股票。按照其時騰訊每股二百元港幣的股價，他們預計拿出了十五億元用作此次獎勵。

當然，騰訊的股價又是一個神話般的傳奇。二○○四年六月十六日，騰訊控股正式掛牌上市，當日以 4.375 港元開盤。十二年後，這個價格累計漲幅超過了二百五十倍。

隨著移動終端的手機的發展，中國成為全世界互聯網包括移動互聯網最普及的國家。在馬化騰的概念中，騰訊在過去五年裡，從封閉的環境變成一個開放的環境，變成一個真正互聯的生態。「內部的一些原有的業務做得不好的砍掉、賣掉、送出去，只保留最核心的通信和數字內容，包括現在提倡的——『互聯網+』，所謂的『+』就是跟其他企業的充分合作。」

按照二千三百多億美元的市值，騰訊已經是亞洲最大的互聯網公司。這個自稱是典型的「程序猿」、原本沒打算開公司的企業家，在很多場合都表現得十分謙遜，面對自己人也不例外，「騰訊十八年來，我更多講的是感恩，感恩所有的同事們。」

實際上，他正手握一個極其驚人的用戶群體和一個龐大的商業帝國。騰訊旗下微信和 QQ 的月活躍用戶數已經分別達到八點零六億和八點九九億。二○一六年，中國大陸總人口也不過十三億八千二百七十一萬人。

他的形象儒雅白淨，且外表溫和，但這位「QQ 之父」一直有很強的開拓力，以及伴隨而來的很深的危機感。媒體評價他十八年來的創業路徑時，必然繞不開敬畏、創新、開放等幾個關鍵詞。

馬化騰說，騰訊發展歷程中遇到了最大的三次困難。

第一次是初期融資期，在發展初期團隊投標失敗、用戶瘋長，沒錢買服務器，這是最難的時候。但這種困難也迫使騰訊團隊從很早就想怎樣有造血的能力。

第二次是跟 MSN 競爭。「別人都認為你死定了，只是什麼時候死而已。最後還是挺住了，我們的產品做得比國外的產品更適合中國人使用。」能贏得與 MSN 之戰主要在於 QQ 結合中國的網絡環境和中國用戶的使用習慣，做了很多優化。

第三個坎是五年前微信誕生之前，新浪微博從社交媒體轉向社交網絡，帶來了很大壓力。

當然，騰訊歷史上最大的危機應該是「3Q 大戰」。奇虎 360 與騰訊間的糾葛由來已久，源於二〇一〇年雙方「明星產品」之間的「互掐」。二〇一〇年九月二十七日，360 發布了其新開發的「隱私保護器」，專門蒐集 QQ 軟件是否侵犯用戶隱私。隨後，QQ 立即指出 360 瀏覽器涉嫌借黃色網站推廣。二〇一〇年十一月三日，騰訊宣布在裝有 360 軟件的電腦上停止運行 QQ 軟件，用戶必須卸載 360 軟件才可登錄 QQ，強迫用戶「二選一」。

為了各自的利益，從二〇一〇年到二〇一四年，兩家公司上演了一系列互聯網之戰，並走上了訴訟之路。

雙方互訴三場，奇虎 360 敗訴。其中奇虎 360 訴騰訊公司壟斷案尤為引人注目，二〇一四年十月十六日上午，最高人民法院判定：認定騰訊旗下的 QQ 並不具備市場支配地位，駁回奇虎 360 的上訴，維持一審法院判決。

馬化騰在當年的十二月五日宣布騰訊進入為期半年的戰略轉型籌備期。他說，「壟斷」是一個令人煩惱的罪名。在很多情況下這是一個假想敵，是一個不存在的東西。回顧二十世紀九〇年代，大家看我們 IT 產業，微軟是給人詬病最多的被指責壟斷的公司。在互聯網時代到來的時候，微軟面臨什麼問題呢？我們看到很多新的公司照樣可以崛起。幾乎不可能所有創新者、創業者都認為毫無希望，微軟可能進入很多領域，把很多產業都占到第一位的時候，那還有什麼機會呢？我們看到，未來發展其實大家都有目共睹，不僅產生了Google，還產生了 eBay，而且像 Google 這麼強大的公司，已經無所不能，所有互聯網產品線都有他的投入。我們看到仍然有Facebook 的崛起，Facebook 之後當人們覺得社交網站在人際關係上已經沒有辦法能夠挑戰他地位的時候，我們又看到一種新的形態，微博的形態崛起。

馬化騰有點委屈地說，「所以，我們看到很多所謂的壟斷，實際上在產業不斷變革的時候，他依然面臨很大的危機。也就是說，在價值變遷迅速的產業裡面，沒有一個公司是可以高枕無憂的。所以說，挑戰像阿里巴巴、百度和騰訊——有人說是三座大山，有效方法不是建立一個類似的平台，形成一個壟斷，而能夠順應而上形成一個好的產業鏈才是一個好的方法。」

「事後回想其實有很多的反思在這裡面，但是我不想沉浸在所有的紛爭之中，我更希望往前走，向前看。」馬化騰說，這個紛爭更加堅定了騰訊去改革，去轉型的一個步伐。「我們希望這是一次慎重、徹底、完整的轉型。」

此後，騰訊相繼把搜索、電商等業務以投資的形式出讓，專注做互聯網公共事業的基礎連接服務。

從模仿，到公敵，
再到大哥的奇妙路徑

　　IT 評論人士評價騰訊的發展路徑時說，「騰訊創辦十八年，走了一條從模仿，到公敵，再到大哥的奇妙路徑。」

　　一九八四年，馬化騰隨父母來到深圳這座城市，從初中到大學都在深圳讀書，畢業後在深圳的一家通信企業工作了六年，開始和初中、大學同班同學，還有一位電信行業的同行，總共五個人一起創業。當時全中國網民才三百萬人。

　　在一九九九年那時，互聯網的發展究竟能給人帶來多大的想像，恐怕並沒有幾個人可以站出來打包票。在整個互聯網發展初期，很多時候互聯網都是被作為技術去應用，很少有人去接觸到。這樣一種存在於技術層面的東西，很難給人一個想像空間。在這種大背景下，馬化騰能夠毅然決然地在買房和創業這個抉擇上，發現互聯網，並且做出了 QQ，這顯然是因為馬化騰本身對於互聯網和 IM（即時通信）具有前瞻性——現在的雷布斯當年甚至也拒絕了對騰訊的投資。

　　你可以說，馬化騰做 QQ 也是出於偶然一做電信相關產品開發的附屬品，但是這顯然不能夠解釋為什麼 QQ 能夠在接下來很短的時間內超越 OICQ——當時 IM 的王牌產品。存儲、個性頭像等等，這些現在我們看起來很普通的產品，在當時的意義可以說是不亞於現在微信的偉大創新。

　　再早一點，或者再晚一點，或許 QQ 都不會獲得成功。正是抓住了中國互聯網剛剛起步的第一波紅利，QQ 為之後的騰訊上市，乃至現在的社交帝國打下了堅實的基礎。

騰訊在創業前階段，準確抓住了幾個重要關頭。

首先是運營商的紅利。QQ 雖然在起步階段就獲得了大量用戶，但是如何賺錢在當時顯然是一個大問題。要知道，當時資本市場對互聯網還是處於非常保守的狀態，也沒有現在的什麼市夢率這一說，融資的擊鼓傳花產業鏈並沒有成熟，企業更沒有說「現階段不考慮贏利」的底氣。這時候，QQ 抓住了運營商這根救命稻草，順勢進行了轉身。

在當時，SP（服務提供商）類業務可以說是最早的互聯網企業賺錢的方式。這對於 QQ 來說，算是救了 QQ 的命，如果沒有這些 SP 業務，QQ 或許真的會以一百萬元被賣掉也未可知。這些收入，不僅讓 QQ 能夠維持自己的運營，同時也為之後的上市打下了基礎一在當時，互聯網企業還是很難在不贏利的狀態下就順利讓資本埋單的。 在做 SP 的同時，QQ 自身也相對比較爭氣。一方面在產品上接連推出了會員、QQ 秀等具備增值收費能力的功能；另一方面也開始發行 Q 幣，這可是到現在為止，唯一可以跟電話卡媲美的硬通貨。儘管 SP 業務最終還是下滑了，但是 QQ 在這一波上，抓住了關鍵，讓自己擺脫了困局。

其次是 PC（個人計算機）應用的爆發期。在二〇〇五年，也就是騰訊上市之後，QQ 幾乎已經成為巨無霸型的產品。而在當時，正是桌面軟件的爆發期，什麼千千靜聽、暴風影音、迅雷、輸入法等等，當時都會被軟件市場列為裝機必備。騰訊在這個時候，利用 QQ 的強大資源導流，開始向同類型的產品進軍，先後出了類似於 QQ 影音、QQ 音樂、QQ 瀏覽器、QQ 輸入法等一系列的產品。儘管在當時遭到了行業的集體吐槽——血輪眼，但從現在來看，騰訊的很多橫向拓展的產品，都是在這一波打下了基礎。比如剛剛獨立出來的 QQ 音樂，以及市場占有率已經排名前幾位的 QQ 瀏覽器，等等。除此之外，QQ 在這個時期也打敗了 MSN，可能很多人不知道，在 MSN 的巔峰時期，其市場占有率是超過 QQ 的。

騰訊還順勢一起推出了門戶網站，在當時三大門戶林立的狀況下，生生靠著 QQ 的資源——mini 彈窗、tips 等等殺出了一條血路，最終和新浪、搜狐、網易並稱為四大門戶。這對於騰訊來說可是有戰略意義的，除了由此可以掌握一定的話語權之外，還為之後的騰訊視頻、騰訊體育等等打下了基礎，門戶的廣告營收在當時對互聯網企業來說是僅次於增值服務的重要營收。QQ 在這個時期內打下的基礎，既為自己之後的發展提供了空間，同時也是進行了戰略性的防禦。

再次是遊戲的窗口。陳天橋的盛大將互聯網拉入了「挖土機掘金」的時代，互聯網企業在增值服務和廣告之後，終於又找到了一個最快也是最大化的賺錢模式。騰訊很幸運地抓住了這個機會，這不僅是當時，更是現在的最重要營收，沒有之一。在當時，騰訊進入遊戲領域其實並沒有那麼順利，前期代理的幾個遊戲都沒有能夠闖出來，甚至默默無聞，直到騰訊發現了棋牌類遊戲，這個由騰訊自主研發的平台，在當時迅速打敗了聯眾成為最熱也是最火的平台。在這裡，QQ 的社交關係鏈真正有了用武之地，也是從此開始，騰訊意識到了社交和遊戲具有天然的匹配度。在棋牌類遊戲成功之後，騰訊推出的一些遊戲類似於 DNF 和後來的 CF 等等，就開始接連成功，一直到現在的 LOL，長期霸占著整個遊戲市場的半壁江山。

最重要的是，騰訊抓住了社交網絡的爆發期。Facebook 的橫空出世給了很多互聯網公司啟發，包括當時的校內網、開心網等一批網站都迅速發展了起來。在當時，這些網站的社交屬性幾乎可以跟 QQ 媲美，一時瑜亮。但 QQ 當時有一個最主要的撒手鐧── QQ 空間。據有關數據，在人人網（原校內網）最鼎盛的時候，它在社交平台的市場和用戶占有率都跟 QQ 空間不在一個檔次。雖然當時的偷菜、移車位等遊戲非常火爆，但是 QQ 空間的迅速跟進，立即就讓用戶進行了轉移。直到現在，很多人都會問一個問題：「為什麼中國沒有出現 Facebook？」其實，當時 QQ 依靠 QQ 空間對人人網和開心網的阻擊，徹底粉碎了中國 Facebook 的夢。QQ 空間的迅速發展，不僅僅是為 QQ 從 IM 過渡到了一個整體的社交平台，更為其之後的 Feeds 廣告打下了基礎一如今在很多企業的眼裡，QQ 空間的 Feeds 廣告都是最優質的資源。

下一個影響世界的
創新會是什麼？

創業初期時，馬化騰完全顧不及什麼是領導力，讓公司活下去才是最重要的。他說：「我父母都沒有想到，我這個書呆子可以開公司。所以第一步就是找合夥人，他們可以彌補我的缺陷。」

他找到的合夥人許晨曄、張志東和陳一丹都是他的中學或大學同學，曾李青則是過去的同事。這幾個人各有所長，互補性強。馬化騰要做的是，「用好每個人的特長，平衡各方意見」。他不是霸道總裁，管理上也不是一言堂。創業早期，騰訊幾個合夥人一人一份雞煲飯，一坐就是兩三個小時，一堆公事也擺上檯面，很多公司的重要戰略決策起源於此。吃雞煲飯是騰訊合夥人文化的一個象徵。甚至在幾個合夥人逐步退出一線管理之後，他們仍保持著良好的互動關係，沒有違和聲音或事件傳出。陳一丹對此的解釋是，幾個合夥人家庭背景相似，導致大家性格相近，比較溫和細緻，能夠接受協商制，而不是追求個人英雄主義。

然而互聯網瞬息萬變，騰訊這座帝國如何保持創新？這是馬化騰必須面對的。

二○一○年，所有人都在爭奪移動互聯網船票，那是非生即死之戰。百度、360 等公司被認為在這波浪潮中沒有拿出真正有影響力的產品而有掉隊風險。騰訊的處境也不樂觀，微博在覬覦社交網絡，從 PC 到移動的轉型中，QQ 的歷史包袱很沉重。馬化騰坦承，這是他們遭遇的最大危機。

當時騰訊內部有三個團隊參與顛覆型的產品研發，誰最先解決手機移動終端問題，誰就勝出。最後 QQ 郵箱團隊開發出一個通過手機快速收發郵件的客戶端產品，快到讓用戶以為不是郵件，這個產品就是後來的微信。它的研發者張小龍因此成為微信之父。

在騰訊，他們早已習慣競爭對象可能就是自己人。馬化騰毫不避諱這點，甚至他覺得內部良性競爭很有必要。「自己打自己才會努力，公司才不會丟失一些大的戰略機會。」

二〇一三年，馬化騰在接受央視對話採訪時稱，他們拿到了一張移動互聯網的站票。二〇一六年六月，他說，還沒等我們坐下來船已經到岸了，要上新大陸了。因為以人工智能為代表的新一波技術浪潮才是未來，包括騰訊在內的互聯網巨頭都在加緊布局。AlphaGo 人機大戰時，馬化騰和團隊都很興奮，這個沉寂多年的技術煥發新機，他們蠢蠢欲動地想做點什麼。

收納了三百五十萬個應用、日分發達二億的應用寶 7.0 版本將新增一個基於 AI（人工智能）和雲端的機器人功能，未來用戶不下載滴滴也可以在應用寶裡叫車。騰訊會基於 AI 做更多技術層面的研發，開放給更多合作夥伴。

即便如此，馬化騰仍然不知道下一個影響世界的創新會是什麼。「每一次大的變革都伴隨著終端的變化，智能手機興起，一切的生態都不一樣。未來隨著 VR（虛擬現實）、AR（增強現實）等終端越來越普及，也會發生新的應用場景變化。」

從上學開始，馬化騰就鍾情天文，雖然這與他創業沒有直接的關係，但是對他思考問題的方式有一定的影響。他說：「喜歡天文會覺得自己很渺小，可能我們在宇宙中從來就是一個偶然。所以遇到什麼事情都覺得沒有什麼大不了的，會讓你想得更開。」

▎藝術家張小龍和微信

在今天，中國人對微信的依賴程度幾乎達到極致。這也是騰訊帝國在新世紀第二個十年最卓越的成就。

馬化騰回憶，當時有三個內部團隊做微信產品，原來QQ有另外一個事業群，有新的機會做手機上的IM讓他們做理所當然。另外移動QQ也在做。所以原先先天的結構不合理，後來迅速做了調整把產品聚攏。各類產品，包括新聞、遊戲原來在PC和移動都是分開的，後來聚攏到一塊。

「另外一個就是在廣州的QQ郵箱的團隊，很早接觸移動辦公。當時我們就想能不能在QQ郵箱開發一個APP，讓每一個員工都能很方便地用手機郵件。當時就讓這個團隊研發手機郵箱，最後微信的機會一出來，就是這個團隊五六個人把手機端的郵件系統改成微信。所以微信其實是一個郵件系統，只是快速的短郵件，後端的服務器就是原先郵箱的團隊。這個團隊用了一個多月就出了一個原型，張小龍帶領這個團隊，也有很強的產品能力。」

「微信剛出來的時候數據不好，起不來，真正的啟動的因素一是語音，國外同類產品沒有這個功能，有這個功能之後迅速火爆；第二是跟手機通訊錄的整合，把通訊錄互相匹配，最開始的啟動是把QQ的關係鏈推過去讓它生存，但是把手機通訊錄導過去會導入很多高端用戶，增加黏性。」

作為至關重要的人物，張小龍看上去皮膚黝黑，是一位愛打高爾夫球的中年男子，也有很多人評價，他在多數時候「扮演著一名藝術家的角色」，「他將產品視為自己所創作的藝術品」。張小龍也在這十七年間，持續地進行著自我迭代與升級。多年前被以一千二百萬元人民幣賣掉的 Foxmail 與其說是他產品上的成功，不如說是商業上的失敗——相比這點金錢，更值得惋惜的是他錯過的巨大商業機會。這就是張小龍 1.0，關鍵詞是產品和技術。在微信初期，他將工具上升為平台，將服務用戶的簡單需求變成引導他們的喜怒哀樂，完成了第二次升級。

一九九八年的秋天，周鴻禕經人引薦第一次在廣州見到了張小龍。他看到這名在業界已是小有名氣的程序員正和十幾個人擠在一間小破辦公室內，周遭煙霧繚繞。看到周鴻禕之後，張小龍掐滅了手上的煙，面無表情地向他走來。張小龍所開發的 Foxmail 已經擁有了二百萬用戶，是國內用戶量最大的共享軟件。而當年周鴻禕還僅是方正軟件研發中心的一名副主任。

周鴻禕說，當年 Foxmail 是沒有商業模式的，他經常批駁張小龍這一點，說要加廣告，要贏利。張小龍說為什麼非要這樣？只要有用戶，有情懷就好了。每一次爭論，都是張小龍以長時間的沉默來結束。「這樣的一個人怎麼就做出了微信呢？」周鴻禕很疑惑。

Foxmail 如日中天時，騰訊不過十萬用戶，多數人認為郵箱是比社交更大的一塊領域。而正當馬化騰、張朝陽欣喜地尋找風投向商業進軍時，張小龍經常獨自一人在深夜看用戶來信，他手不離開鍵盤，一直按著下箭頭，看著一封封信從眼前流過，每封信的停留時間不超過一秒。在張小龍眼裡，Foxmail 已經變成了一個大包袱，每天都有無數的人催促他往前跑，而龐大的知名度和用戶量，並沒有給他帶來任何經濟上或社會地位上的好處。

一年後，張小龍選擇將 Foxmai 拙售給了一家並不知名的互聯網公司博大。消息宣布後的夜晚，他寫下了一封充滿傷感情緒的信，他在信中將 Foxmail 比喻為他精心雕塑的藝術品。「從靈魂到外表，我能數出它每一個細節，每一個典故。在我的心中，它是有靈魂的，因為它的每一段代碼，都有我那一刻塑造它時的意識。我突然有了一種想反悔的衝動。」

藝術家張小龍一直是孤獨的創作者，過去他走得很順，直到這條寬闊的賽道中出現了障礙物——商業和贏利。傲游、千千靜聽、超級兔子等無數共享軟件都被撞飛了，張小龍則僥倖進入了另一條跑道。當年他剛過三十一歲，但很多人認為他的個人傳奇似乎就此終結。

那年夏天，百度在納斯達克上市，所有人都以為自己眼花了——百度股價從發行價 27 美元飆升至 122.54 美元，當天暴漲 354%，人們看到了資本和商業的力量。張小龍則帶著博大給他的收購款，買了輛車，去了一直想去的西藏。

「怎麼說呢，這個人，太單純。」周鴻禕說。這名在商界以狡黠善戰而著稱的企業家，這樣評價比他還大一歲的張小龍。

錯過了互聯網衝擊納斯達克的第一波高潮後，博大走向沒落。二〇〇五年，張小龍和 Foxmail 被打包出售給了騰訊。張小龍在騰訊接手了 QQ 郵箱，並帶領著 QQ 郵箱超越網易郵箱成為中國最大的郵件服務商，但這只是他再一次證明了自己的產品能力而已。

在很多時代，有力量的都是商人，多數藝術家都無法擺脫被商人供養而無法自主的命運。Foxmail 給張小龍帶來的是巨大的聲望，以及顛沛流離的生活。張小龍身邊一直圍繞著商人，他和商人做朋友，甚至想去微軟學習如何進行商業運作，但最終沒有在商業上邁出一步。最後，他身邊的大多兼具產品與商業天分的朋友都成功了，雷軍、周鴻禕、馬化騰，甚至當年採訪他的記者李學凌。

有人評價，張小龍始終是一個趕潮的人，但他不在潮中。從一名程序員到一名產品經理，他學會了掌控自己的產品，但他始終無法掌控用戶。然而慷慨的命運給了他第三次機會，而這次成功來得太大、太快了。

曾鳴是微信十三名創始團隊成員之一，他說當時包括張小龍在內的所有人都不知道要把微信做成什麼樣，更何況這些成員中還有一半是毫無經驗的實習生。他們最初的目標是又快又穩定——這和張小龍當年做 Foxmail 的思路如出一轍，是一種單純的做工具的思路。如果張小龍的產品觀只是停留於此，那麼他做出來的充其量只是一款還不錯的聊天工具。

還有同事將張小龍比喻為一名想拍出完美大片的導演，他不是不能接受廣告的植入，而是不能容忍生硬的植入，因為生硬會破壞完美。吳毅曾是財付通的助理總經理，他描述，三年前第一次見張小龍，張就在思考如何用支付聯繫微信和商業。「他並不排斥完美的合作，比如 QQ 音樂、QQ 郵箱、支付。」

微信早期，張小龍負責產品，而如何接入第三方商戶，如何拓展線上到線下等商業化規則，由騰訊電商副總裁戴志康負責，就連支付也是交予財付通團隊來做。二〇一二年底，Pingwest 創始人駱軼航撰文說，微信商業化過慢的癥結在於張與戴之間的內部分歧。

在此之後發生的戴志康離職，微信支付從財付通剝離併入微信，以及微信事業群的獨立等一系列事件，你或許可以看作張小龍已有了選擇——既然微信商業化不可避免，那就由微信團隊自己來主導商業化。這同時也意味著以馬化騰、劉熾平為代表的騰訊高層作出了選擇，他們選擇將商業化交給張小龍，並賦予他全權。

對內把握商業化的控制權。對外，他試圖建立一整套新的體系來處理好藝術和商業的關係。舉例說，騰訊內部曾有一百二十個項目在排隊接入微信，而微信的要求是先跑一個半月的數據，然後按照數據篩選。

「微信把開通什麼功能，接入什麼合作對像這些商業行為納入到了產品的一部分，而對於大多數人來說，產品是商業的一部分。」一位騰訊內部高層人士說，你可以將之理解為商業化的價值觀，以及藝術家的方法論。

即便到了今天，微信的商業策略也被認為是相對保守的。一名業內人士評價，張小龍對待商業化正在經歷一個從逃避到試探到主導再到適應的過程，他從不把話說滿，做不到的他肯定不說，做得到的他也不見得會說。

微信的商業化承載了整個騰訊轉型的大理想。從目前來看，它被分為了三大步－增值服務、電商和 O2O。現在它只完成了第一步，而公眾號則可以讓微信同時實現後兩步。曾鳴說，未來微信會開放更多的入口，也會提供所有商家所期待的流量入口。

評論家們曾經以為微信只是導流的工具，而現在微信藉助公眾號，將騰訊強大的線上營銷能力和線下商業進行連接，構建了一個龐大的線上+線下生態，在這個生態中將誕生電商、O2O、健康等各種小生態。微信和 QQ 的差別從某種程度上來說正如實體經濟對陣虛擬經濟，而後者只是前者的 7% 不到。

過去張小龍習慣站在商人後面，而現在他到了第一線，走上了馬化騰走過的那條路——同時做產品和商業的引領者。但商業的利益重大而複雜，所以在很長一段時間內，可以想像，張小龍還會選擇繼續沉默。

　　馬化騰回憶，最開始微信推出的時候，運營商很緊張了，沒人發短信，電話也少了。「我要限制你，全世界有很多國家會出很多招去限制你。其實這個是勢不可擋，我一直跟他們說你們放心，你們絕對會受益的，你們的語音業務下降了，但是你的流量上去了，怎麼會吃虧呢？增長很難說，直到去年，數據增長比語音快，現在放心了，跟我是魚和水的關係。」

「傳祺」，
傳奇！

進軍美國之心和
一輛叫 GS8 的車

　　第一輛傳祺車在七年前從廣州的工廠下線。當時，新世紀進入第二個十年，私家車的市場在中國正變得越來越大。

　　如今，這個在中國銷量第六的汽車品牌在二〇一七年的底特律車展上成為該車展歷史上首個進入主展館的中國品牌。觀察家認為，它進入美國市場的主要挑戰，是與測試和滿足全球最高安全及排放標準相關的高成本。「美國有著比中國嚴格太多的規則。」

　　廣汽集團的業績正在變得越來越漂亮：二〇一六年，連續第四年入圍《財富》世界五百強，位居第三百零三名，比上一年排名上升了五十九位。

　　在全球的範圍內，自主創新能力已經成為區域競爭力的突出體現。今天，廣東的高新技術企業數量躍居全國首位，新舊動能轉換取得成效。汽車自主品牌廣汽傳祺的成功，就是廣東汽車工業成績單上最閃耀的一頁。

　　廣汽集團從二〇〇五年開始謀劃自主品牌，到目前累計投資一百三十億元，建成了國內一流的研發中心和世界級的整車及發動機工廠，推出了廣汽傳祺自主品牌。在 J.D.Power 發布的二〇一五中國新車質量研究報告（IQS）中，廣汽傳祺連續三年蟬聯中國品牌品質冠軍，排名第八，與廣汽豐田齊名。在銷量上，廣汽傳祺從二〇一一年進入市場，銷量呈跨越式增長，二〇一一年 1.7 萬輛，二〇一四年11.6 萬輛。二〇一五年中國汽車市場同比增長僅 4.7%，廣汽傳祺的銷量達十九萬輛，同比增長 63%，全年實現銷售收入 177 億元，而傳祺首款SUV-GS4 的月銷量躋身全國 SUV 前三名。據瞭解，在廣汽集團啟動實施的「十三五」戰略規劃中，提出了「一五一三」戰略，其中「一」個重點就是舉全集團之力發展自主品牌，實現自主品牌事業的跨越式發展。

二〇一六年，廣汽傳祺取得銷量和品牌的「雙突破」。二〇一七年一月，廣汽傳祺延續上一年良好勢頭，繼續保持增長態勢。一月份，廣汽傳祺累計銷售 46273 輛，同比增長 60%，增幅位居國內汽車主機廠之首，刷新中國本土品牌新高度。其中，上市僅三個月的「旗艦級豪華大七座 SUV」──傳祺 GS8，一月份共售出 9418 輛，連續三個月大幅增長。

傳祺 GS8 單月銷量 9418 輛，與豐田漢蘭達、福特銳界並肩，形成三強鼎立的中大型 SUV 市場格局。這是中國本土品牌第一次在與合資對手直面對決當中，表現出堅挺的姿態。傳祺 GS8 在十六萬至二十五萬元這一中國本土品牌從未染指的價格區間成功立足，這在中國汽車歷史上，同樣是第一次。

按照如此高的發展速度，傳祺 GS8 有望超越漢蘭達和銳界，在細分市場中衝擊第一。現在看 GS8 的銷售勢頭，也是奔著這個「小目標」去的。一旦實現，無疑是可以載入中國汽車史冊的事件，讓所有為中國汽車崛起而奮鬥三十餘年的汽車人為之振奮，也為後來者堅定信心。

不僅如此，傳祺 GS8 的熱銷，讓廣汽傳祺徹底擺脫「一條腿」走路的尷尬。熱銷車型從一款增至兩款，產品結構趨於合理，車型售價區間進一步擴大。並助推廣汽傳祺在廣汽集團總銷量比重從

22.38%提升至 27.55%，提高 5 個百分點，逼近 30%大關。

以 GS8 熱銷為標誌，廣汽傳祺正在引領廣東汽車業從「廣東製造」邁向「廣東創造」，將「中國製造」的影響力從產品躍升至品牌。在不遠的將來，隨著廣汽傳祺海外戰略的逐步推進，尤其是二〇一九年正式登陸美國市場，還將助推「中國品牌」影響力從中國市場擴大到全球市場。「廣汽傳祺將成為中國汽車領軍品牌，年產銷一百萬輛會比最初預計的二〇二〇年提前實現。」在二〇一七年北美底特律車展前夜，廣汽集團執行委員會副主任、廣汽乘用車公司總經理郁俊信心滿滿地直言。

傳祺 GS8 的出現絕非偶然，沒有任何僥倖的成分，這來源於廣汽傳祺堅持高端的發展戰略，堅持正向開發，堅持國際標準。從剛開始的 GA5，再到 GS5、GS4，傳祺一直是平均單車價格最高的本土汽車品牌，平均單車售價甚至高於一些合資品牌。傳祺 GS8 到來之前，廣汽傳祺 GS4 平均單車售價約為十四萬元。GS8 到來之後，廣汽傳祺將平均單車售價一舉提升到接近二十萬元的嶄新高度，為後續車型贏得寬闊的戰略空間。

自亮相以來，傳祺 GS8「超硬朗霸氣外觀」的造型設計，獲得媒體與消費者一致好評。然而，出色的外觀設計，僅是 GS8 取得如此出色成績的一方面原因。傳祺 GS8 還提供「全地形無畏駕控」「大格局七座空間」「新視野智能互聯」，以及全面超越同級的品質與性價比優勢，全面領先用戶期待。

上市以來，傳祺 GS8 接連斬獲「年度中國品牌 SUV」「年度最具實力大型 SUV」「二〇一六十大強烈推薦新車獎」「年度人氣 SUV」等國內外近百項大獎，受到權威媒體和業界的廣泛讚譽，實現了銷量和口碑雙豐收。

與此同時，在 J.D.Power 中國新車質量研究報告中，傳祺品牌已經連續四年蟬聯中國品牌第一，品質超越了絕大部分合資產品，消費者的普遍信賴成為傳祺產品熱銷的內在因素。

在消費升級市場趨勢中，品牌力和車型品質在汽車企業競爭中發揮的作用日益關鍵。傳祺 GS8 全面搭載廣汽傳祺在研發、設計、製造等領域的創新成果。

在中國市場，只要打開二十萬至二十五萬元這一價位的市場，就獲得全價格區間的市場通行證。豐田、本田都是在凱美瑞和雅閣熱銷而確定其全球主流汽車主機廠的江湖地位。傳祺 GS8 的成功之於廣汽傳祺，也是具有里程碑式的意義。傳祺 GS8 之後，廣汽傳祺上可以進入豪華車市場，與謳歌、英菲尼迪、凱迪拉克競爭，往下可以在 B 級、A+級、A 級、A0 級等各個細分市場大展拳腳。

廣汽傳祺不是第一個決心堅持高端的中國品牌，當然也不是最後一個。過去十年，中國汽車走一條曲曲折折的彎路，事實證明，「品牌向上」和「堅持正向研發」才是中國本土汽車品牌應該努力的方向。進入所有標準苛刻的中高端市場，在某種程度上，就是向所有消費者展示自己的能力。

GS8 將中國本土汽車品牌一乃至中國製造一拔擢到新的高度。這種高度，不是來自於虛高的定價，也非口頭的吹噓，是實實在在的訂單，和真真切切的銷量數字。在十六萬至二十五萬元這個價格區間，三個月實現四萬張訂單，和 9418 輛的月銷量，不能說後無來者，但至少在此前，是沒有先例的。

「中國製造」的代表，是科技界的華為，也是以格力、海爾為首的家電企業。要拼齊「中國製造」完整的版圖，必須得有汽車企業。在汽車企業中實現全力衝刺並衝線，一個國家製造業的形象才能在全球範圍內樹立起來。世界汽車製造業在迎來英國、美國、德國、日本、韓國之後，隨著以廣汽傳祺為首的中國汽車品牌的崛起，也將迎來中國品牌的身影。

技術創新沒有捷徑

沿著「傳祺」生產線一路參觀，彷彿置身於一個科幻的世界：機器人揮動巨大的手臂精確銲接、裝配，無人駕駛推車將各種部件準確送到工位；這一端一個個空的車殼子魚貫而入，那一端一輛輛嶄新的「傳祺」整車魚貫而出……

對於「傳祺」含義的解釋，廣汽集團董事長曾慶洪說，祺是吉祥、幸福的意思，我們要讓自主品牌汽車向所有用戶傳遞吉祥和幸福。

然而要實現這個美好的祝願並不容易。「『傳祺』剛上馬的時候，我的內心是崩潰的。」廣汽集團副總經理、乘用車公司董事長吳松一直具體負責傳祺系列產品的生產與銷售，在廣汽其他幾個合資品牌廣汽本田、廣汽豐田等賺得盆滿缽滿的時候，起步階段的「傳祺」卻連續數年巨額虧損。市場對自主品牌汽車質量與性能的天生不信任，他還只是窩火；集團內部兄弟單位的冷嘲熱諷就讓他哭笑不得了——你們誰不好好幹，發配你們去「傳祺」。

面對合資品牌一統市場的巨大壓力，自主品牌汽車竟真的不能在全球最大且高速發展的國內市場上贏得一席之地？對此他們主動調低「傳祺」產銷任務，但不惜一切狠抓產品質量。曾慶洪說，「傳祺」品牌是靠品質打出來的，沒有「品」就沒有「牌」，「傳祺」首要的是不惜一切抓產品品質，他就不相信「傳祺」品牌打不出來。

經過多年刻苦努力，走過了自主品牌汽車最艱難的市場啟動期，廣汽傳祺開始以優異的品質和高性價比逐步走進千家萬戶。二〇一六年一至十月，廣汽傳祺全系銷量二十九點六萬輛，同比增長百分之一百二十六，發展速度和贏利水平位居中國汽車品牌前列。

在廣汽自主品牌汽車剛上馬的時候，無論是業內還是普通消費者幾乎沒人看好，因為「傳祺」當時沒有人才、沒有資金、沒有技術，有人開玩笑說這是一個「三無」公司。最關鍵的問題是，廣汽沒有整車設計與研發能力。連整車都不能設計，談什麼自主品牌？

但誰也沒有料到，廣汽能投入一百多億元建成國際先進的汽車研究院，從二〇〇六年成立時僅有三四十名研發人員，到今天已建立起一支三千餘人的研發人才隊伍。目前這裡擁有整車、動力總成、新能源等十餘個先進實驗室和含銲接、塗裝、總裝、機加工在內的試制工廠，以及汽車調校專用試驗跑道，具備整車整機及關鍵部件研發、試制、試驗能力。這些都為廣汽傳祺提供了源源不斷的發展力。「廣汽研究院一年可以推出五個新車型。」廣汽研究院副院長張帆介紹說。

從沒有整車開發能力到新車型推出一批，研發一批，儲備一批，廣汽研究院已經向市場推出一系列車型，實現產品全覆蓋。「廣汽研究院的成功和自主品牌整車設計能力的提升說明，技術創新沒有捷徑，必須一步一個腳印。」曾慶洪說。

「自主品牌汽車不會一帆風順，但我始終相信未來中國汽車市場一定是自主品牌汽車主導，中國自主品牌汽車也一定能走向世界。」作為我國汽車工業崛起全過程的見證者和參與者，曾慶洪表示，不僅是普通的乘用車和商用車，新能源汽車領域更是充滿前景。

新能源汽車一直都被寄予厚望，然而這個研發過程也是相當曲折。「一大筆錢投下去，沒有什麼明顯起色，甚至只能證實此路不通，心裡的滋味相當複雜。」曾慶洪表示。但他相信，新能源汽車一定能像現在的普通汽車一樣走進千家萬戶。

▌「研發外腦」馬可的故事

Marco Mario Gilardi（馬可・馬里奧・吉拉爾迪）的辦公室位於番禺化龍鎮廣汽研究院內。作為廣汽研究院首席專業總師，馬可全程參與了廣汽集團首款自主品牌轎車「傳祺」的研發工作，發揮重要作用。廣東省汽車工程學會理事長、廣汽研究院原院長黃向東形容馬可在傳祺開發中的重要性就像桌子的一條腿：「一張桌子有四條腿，缺失了一條，那就麻煩了，站不住。」

像馬可這樣的「外腦」在廣東還有很多，近年來，外國專家的引進成為廣東人才引進的「重頭戲」。廣東省統計局發布的數據顯示，二〇一四、二〇一五年廣東聘請境外來中國大陸工作專家分別為 13.21 萬人次和 12.99 萬人次，分別占全國比重為 21.3%和 20.8%，聘請境外專家人數居全國第一位。這些外國專家用自己的熱情和專業為廣東的創新驅動發展貢獻力量。

「十一五」之初，廣州提出要生產自主品牌的汽車。二〇〇六年七月，廣汽集團以原廣州汽車技術中心為基礎，成立了廣汽研究院，專門負責廣州自主品牌汽車的研發。原華南理工大學教授、廣汽集團副總經理黃向東出任首任院長。

剛成立的廣汽研究院，除了三個服務部門，僅有四個技術部門，研發人員三十餘人，而且多數是經驗欠缺的年輕人，要自主研發出自己的汽車十分不易，招攬人才成為首要任務。就在這個時候，黃向東在意大利都靈遇到了二十五年未見的老朋友馬可。

「在廣汽和菲亞特的一個合作項目中我見到了一些從廣東來的

人，仔細一看，居然是黃向東！」談起兩個人的再次相遇，馬可說這是一種緣分。

二十世紀八〇年代，黃向東曾在菲亞特研究中心工作，那時馬可剛剛畢業進入菲亞特，二人就在同一間辦公室。再相遇時，馬可已在菲亞特工作了近三十年，而黃向東回國後也一直深耕汽車行業，先後在華南理工大學擔任教授、在廣汽集團擔任副總經理，然後又被授命組建廣汽研究院。

當時，菲亞特有業務在中國，馬可常常到中國出差，對中國的印象很好。黃向東向他講述研發自主品牌汽車的想法，他就常常過來「友情客串」，對年輕的研究人員給予一些技術上的指點。「當時的廣汽研究院非常小，場地也沒有，只在華南理工大學租了一層樓，馬可完全是出於幫助老同事、老朋友，常常過來『客串指導』。」當年在意大利工作時，黃向東就對馬可的人品非常讚賞。

二〇〇七年十二月和二〇〇八年四月，經過多番艱苦談判和細節磋商，廣汽集團先後與菲亞特有關方面簽訂了發動機和底盤平台技術轉讓合同。馬可被調到該公司負責對口廣汽的業務。這個時候，廣州打造自主品牌汽車的思路已相當明確，並進入實質性準備階段，對人才的渴求更甚。黃向東想到直接將馬可「挖」到廣汽。

「你願意來廣汽工作嗎？」黃向東問馬可。馬可用他一貫的幽默作答：「為什麼我們合作這麼久你才問這個問題？」

離開工作二十九年的菲亞特，將妻子獨自留在意大利，馬可說「在這裡找到了激情和目標」。面對黃向東拋過來的橄欖枝，馬可雖然有意，但仍有猶豫。馬可在菲亞特已經工作了近三十年，職位不低，本可安安穩穩做到退休。而且當時兩個女兒已長大成人，出國發展，如果他再離開，妻子將孤身一人留在意大利。對他來說，離鄉背井來中國並非易事。

菲亞特也對其進行了挽留。「有人跟我說，菲亞特當時已經引進了克萊斯勒公司，如果你想有一些海外工作經驗，也可以去克萊斯勒公司。」而且，與克萊斯勒公司相比，當時的廣汽在國際上只是個名不見經傳的小公司。

不過，馬可最終還是選擇了廣汽。很多人不理解他的選擇。但他自己形容為「聽從內心的選擇」。「我突然發現，我這 29 年都在菲亞特度過，我不想再繼續了。」馬可覺得，自己需要有一個新的挑戰、新的轉折，「如果在菲亞特按部就班，我覺得也是不錯的，但我總覺得如果自己足夠好的話，來到中國也能幹出一番新天地。」

「在之前的合作中，我對廣汽產生了好感，因為在這裡我找到了激情和目標。」講述起當年的選擇時，馬可說他是被廣汽的氛圍和廣汽員工的激情所感染。「在和廣汽員工接觸之後，我越來越覺得這裡的年輕人很有激情去把這個事情做好。這裡的領導也有決心去做一個最大最強的汽車行業領軍企業。所以我對這裡的人和事，越來越有好感和興趣。」過去的積累也給了馬可很好的儲備，「我希望有一個從零開始的機會，翻開新的篇章，但也可以說不是從零開始，因為我以前也有了很好的積累。」

一開始什麼都沒有，連底盤都沒有，研發出首款自主品牌，馬可的重要性就像一張桌子不可或缺的那一條腿。二〇〇九年十一月，馬可加盟廣汽。這時的廣汽條件仍然簡陋，甚至連實驗室都沒建起來。而當時廣州的目標是：要在二〇一〇年廣州舉辦的亞運會上，讓來賓坐上廣汽自主品牌汽車。廣州市相關領導將其作為「廣州市自主創新一號工程」。

一開始，很多人覺得這是一個「不可能的任務」。馬可上任後，開始帶領年輕的團隊向目標進發。他主要負責整車集成和車輛底盤兩個環節的研發。為了順利完成任務，馬可週末幾乎都不休息，還要到外地做實驗。「在襄陽，我們做整車實驗，在包頭做沙地實驗，在黑龍江做冰雪實驗。」

當然，他的團隊都是這樣的節奏。「其實週末加班的並不只是我自己，我們有很多人都這樣。我工作，他們也工作，不是我推著他們，而是他們推著我。」兩年內研發出首款自主品牌汽車，困難當然不小。用黃向東的話說，一開始什麼都沒有，連底盤都沒有。但是，這個團隊克服了重重困難。二〇一〇年九月，廣州亞運會前夕，廣汽集團首款自主品牌轎車「傳祺」終於下線，實現了廣州人多年的汽車「自主夢」。

按計畫，五百輛傳祺轎車作為第十六屆亞運會官方指定用車，為來自亞洲及世界各地的貴賓提供服務。「這整個過程中，都有馬可的身影。」黃向東說。

「我的團隊剛開始很弱，都沒有經驗，就需要有人帶。這個關鍵時候，需要頂樑柱。馬可就是頂樑柱之一。」黃向東說，當隊伍慢慢成長起來後，他的頂樑柱的作用仍然存在。「這個團隊要行，這個團隊的核心團隊就必須行，馬可就是核心團隊中最出色的成員之一。」二〇一四年九月，中國政府授予馬可外國人士最高榮譽獎項的——國家「友誼獎」；二〇一五年四月，馬可成功入選國家第四批「外專千人計畫」。不過，馬可並不認為自己是「導師」的角色。「我從來不教他們什麼東西，我只是和他們一起工作。」他說。

　　廣東引進外國專家已成常態。省外國專家局提供的數據顯示，五年來，每年來粵工作的境外專家超過十三萬人次，占全國五分之一，居於首位；累計引進海外人才三點七萬人，其中諾貝爾獎獲得者、發達國家院士、終身教授等一百二十九人，入選中央「外專千人計畫」十九人。如何才能用好這些「外腦」，讓他們為廣東的創新驅動更好地服務？黃向東認為，首先是外在氛圍，要有吸引人的優惠條件。他認為，無論是廣東省還是廣州市，現在都不缺優惠條件了。

　　「但也有很多企業，人才來了也發揮不好，很多時候就是因為不被信任。」曾引進多位外國專家的黃向東說，要用好「外腦」，真正的人才來了之後要能夠被信任，要有委以重任的平台，使其長期、穩定地發揮作用。「現在很多企業，引進的人才總是幹不了多久就走了，什麼原因？那一定是企業在文化、在信任上出了問題。別人幹得不開心啊，或者在這裡幹不了什麼實事。」

　　「另外，比如說，高層次的專家通常和我們一般員工不是一個薪酬體系。如果他來了以後，員工都不喜歡他，覺得他拿那麼多錢還不如我，這也是個問題。」黃向東認為，優化配置是一門藝術，也一門技術，「關鍵是這個企業的主要領導如何看待人才，如何真心真意用人才、愛人才。」

　　「人才有優點，有缺點。他一方面很強，一方面很弱。要容忍他弱的一面，發揮他特長的一面。不能想著利用利用人家，不當作自己人，這樣肯定發揮不了人才的作用。」黃向東說。

廣東「無人機」
翱翔全球天空

▍進入迪拜的億航傳奇

　　這個消息迅速攀登上很多主流媒體的頭版，被很多人稱為「廣東的驕傲」。迪拜當地媒體 Arabian Business 二月十三日援引迪拜交通局的聲明報導稱，「億航 184」在乘客座位前面配有觸摸屏，乘客在地圖上選擇目的地後，無人機將按預設航路飛抵目的地。飛行實際上受地面控制中心監測和控制。迪拜民航局已經頒發了試飛許可，阿聯酋電信負責提供無人機和地面控制中心之間通信的 4G 數據網絡。

　　英國媒體 BBC（英國廣播公司）在十四日報導此事時，援引英國西英格蘭大學航空專家懷特（Steve Wright）博士的觀點稱：真實載人飛行前，飛機要進行一千小時以上的無人飛行測試。

　　廣東的無人機，正在呈現著「翱翔全球天空」的光榮和夢想。繼大疆一騎絕塵地占領全球消費級無人機市場之後，行業應用的技術也在出海。除了億航的載人飛行器，同樣位於廣州的極飛科技率先在日本設立分公司，投入日本的農業植保領域中。撇開無人機玩具，無人機的海外走俏可以說是產業級取勝，是高附加值的製造業的一次輸出。

　　二〇一六年一月在美國，「億航 184」在國際消費類電子產品展覽會上首秀，號稱全球首款低空中短途自動駕駛載人飛行器。「184」意指一名乘客、八個螺旋槳、四支外伸機臂。億航公司官網介紹稱，淨重二百四十千克的「億航 184」使用純電動力，海平面續航時間可達二十五分鐘，平均巡航速度六十千米/小時，最高設計飛行高度是海拔三千五百米。該無人機額定載重一百千克，後備箱容量為可放入一個十八吋行李箱。此外，「億航184」還設有獨立密匙為通信系統進行數據加密。

公開資料顯示，廣州億航由胡華智、熊逸放創始於二〇一四年。當年十二月獲得由 GGV 紀源資本領投的一千萬美元 A 輪融資，又在二〇一五年八月獲得四千二百萬美元的 B 輪融資。目前公司團隊約三百人。

一個航模迷、技術控，一個曾留學海外，還有一個擅長營銷，二〇一四年，三個創業者在廣州相遇，一家名叫億航的無人機公司在天河誕生。從此，這家代表著廣州的無人機公司異軍突起蓬勃發展。

二〇一四年，從美國杜克大學畢業回國創業的熊逸放，在北京遇到了正在向投資人展示無人機的胡華智。當年正是無人機風生水起的一年，位於深圳的無人機領軍企業大疆，在全球商用無人機市場中占有近 70% 的市場份額，而越來越多的廠商開始進入無人機領域，小米、騰訊等互聯網企業更是多次傳出跨界做無人機的消息。而彼時的廣州，正是無人機發展的空白地。

當熊逸放又認識了銷售人才楊鎮全後，三人一拍即合，二〇一四年，他們在廣州開始了億航的創業之路。他們瞄準「傻瓜式」無人機操作市場開發產品，在手機上安裝一個 APP 即可輕鬆地操控無人機飛行，還可以讓無人機自動跟隨用戶。

站在無人機產業風口上的億航，像火箭一樣快速躍升，成立僅半年多就融資一千萬美元，估值在六個月之內翻了二十五倍，還被美國雜誌《快公司》評為二〇一四中國年度最創新公司五十強，位列第二。楊鎮全說，廣州是國際化的貿易大都會，而且政策和供應鏈等都非常符合做硬件的環境，他們非常感謝這片創新創業熱土，給了億航「飛一般」的成長速度。

二〇一七年的元宵節，廣州在海心沙創造了一項浪漫的吉尼斯紀錄——一千架無人機編隊花式表演，似漫天飛舞的流星，直升百米夜空。它們「畫」出金雞報曉、喜迎新年、祖國河山等光影佳作，當場創造了「數量最多的無人機編隊飛行表演」吉尼斯世界紀錄。這場「千機變」表演，就是來自億航的「廣州智造」。

元宵節當晚，當時鐘指向九時。「起飛」，對講機中倒計時聲音剛落，廣州交響樂團的六十位藝術家們的指間流淌出著名交響樂《黃河‧第三樂章》，一千架型號為 GHOSTDRONE2.0 的智能航拍機伴隨著音樂冉冉升起。與海心沙隔江相望的花城廣場上人頭攢動，觀眾齊齊仰頭觀看目不轉睛，一幕幕「天幕流星」花式映月，帶來了最夢幻的體驗。在這場表演背後，億航在兩年前就開始研發無人機編隊表演技術，決定採用編隊無人機實時通信網絡，確保即使單個無人機出現故障或受到通信干擾時，都不會影響整體任務的完成。

本次破吉尼斯紀錄的最大亮點，是後台只需一個人、一台電腦、一鍵控制。技術人員說，二〇一六年央視春節聯歡晚會中廣州分會場進行的無人機編隊表演，其實是從全國各地邀請了許多頂尖飛手，用遙控器控制其飛行，降低技術難度和風險。如今表演陣隊達到了一千架，地面也不可能讓一千名飛手實地操控。因此，工程師們設計出一套智能高效的無人機編隊遠程操控系統，會同一時間告訴每一架飛機該怎麼飛、位置在哪兒、隊列如何切換、燈光顏色如何變化等。

　　二〇一七年，全世界的「朋友圈」都被各種無人機編隊飛行表演刷屏。二〇一七年央視春晚，無人機身影再次出現，一款口袋無人機在《滿城煙花》節目中，完成了高難度的室內舞台大型編隊飛行，成為整個春晚科技流的顏值和實力擔當。國際科技公司都將無人機視為利器，大舉進軍文化娛樂產業，樹立良好的品牌形象。

　　從二〇一六年央視春節聯歡晚會中廣州分會場一炮而紅，到二〇一六年夏季達沃斯論壇開幕前夕，三十六架無人機在世界經濟論壇創始人兼主席克勞斯‧施瓦布一行前翩翩起舞，到如今的創吉尼斯世界紀錄，都說明了廣州以科技元素打造「智造」城市的渴望。中國作為無人機產業發展最為如火如荼的市場，廣州也成為目前最為耀眼的無人機舞台。

對天空極度痴迷的汪滔

　　除了廣州億航，廣東還有一位無人機巨頭——深圳大疆。大疆無人機的產品占據了全球民用小型無人機約百分之七十的市場份額，其銷售市場主要集中在歐美國家，占其過去總銷售額的百分之八十。全球無人機行業第一位億萬富翁是一位叫汪滔的中國人。這是《福布斯》雜誌下的定義，汪滔就是大疆的老闆。

　　大疆現在一年可以售出了幾十萬架無人機——許多是其主力機型「大疆精靈」（Phantom）系列。在二〇〇九年至二〇一四年間，大疆的銷售額以每年兩到三倍的速度增長。二〇一五年五月，大疆從 Accel Partners 那裡獲得了七千五百萬美元投資，而持有公司約百分之四十五股份的汪滔的個人資產將達到接近四十億美元。

　　全球的目光都在關注這家公司。無人機在大規模用於商用：在金球獎頒獎典禮上，無人機實時傳送航拍畫面；在尼泊爾 7.8 級大地震中，救援人員依靠無人機來繪製受災地區的地圖；美國愛荷華州的農場主還利用無人機監測麥田；Facebook 將利用自有無人機產品向非洲農場地區提供無線互聯網接入；大疆的無人機還出現在《權力的遊戲》和最新一部《星球大戰》電影的拍攝現場。

　　汪滔的辦公室門上寫著兩行漢字——「只帶腦子」和「不帶情緒」。這位大疆的掌門人遵守著這些規則，他是一位言辭激烈卻相當理性的領導人，每週工作八十多個小時，辦公桌旁邊放著一張單人床。

　　汪滔出生於一九八〇年，他對天空的痴迷始於小學，在讀了一本講述紅色直升機探險故事的漫畫書之後，他開始對天空充滿了想像。在汪滔十六歲的時候，他在一次考試中得了高分，父母為此獎勵了他一架夢寐以求的遙控直升機。然而，他不久便將這個複雜的東西弄壞了，幾個月後才收到從香港發來的用於更換的零部件。

由於成績不是那麼的出類拔萃，汪滔考取美國一流大學的夢想也破滅了。當時，汪滔最想上的大學是麻省理工學院和斯坦福大學，但在申請遭到拒絕後，他只好退而求其次，選擇了香港科技大學，在那裡學習電子工程專業。在上大學的頭三年，汪滔一直沒找到自己的人生目標，但在大四的時候他開發了一套直升機飛行控制系統，他的人生由此改變。

為了這最後一個小組項目，汪滔可謂付出了一切，甚至不惜逃課，還熬夜到凌晨五點。雖然他開發的這個機載計算機的懸停功能在班級展示前一晚出了問題，但他付出的心血並沒有白費。香港科技大學機器人技術教授李澤湘（Li Zexiang）慧眼識珠，發現了汪滔的領導才能以及對技術的理解能力。

於是，在他的引薦下，這個性格倔強的學生讀上了研究生。「汪滔是否比別人更聰明，這我倒是不清楚。」李澤湘說，「但是，學習成績優異的人不見得在工作中就表現得非常突出。」李澤湘是大疆的早期顧問及投資者，現在則是該公司董事會主席，持有百分之十的股份。

汪滔最初在大學宿舍中製造飛行控製器的原型，二〇〇六年他和自己的兩位同學來到了中國製造業中心──深圳。他們在一套三居室的公寓中辦公，汪滔將他在大學獲得的獎學金的剩餘部分全部拿出來搞研究。

隨著核心團隊的建立，汪滔繼續開發產品，並開始向國外業餘愛好者銷售，這些人從德國和新西蘭等國家給他發來電子郵件。在美國，《連線》雜誌主編安德森創辦了無人機愛好者的留言板 DIY Drones，上面的一些用戶提出無人機應該從單旋翼設計向四旋翼設計轉變，因為四旋翼飛行器價格更便宜，也更容易進行編程。因此，大疆開始開發具有自動駕駛功能的更為先進的飛行控製器。開發完成以後，汪滔帶著它們到一些小型貿易展上推銷，比如二〇一一年在印第安納州曼西市舉辦的無線電遙控直升機大會。

　　到二〇一二年晚些時候，大疆已經擁有了一款完整無人機所需要的一切元素：軟件、螺旋槳、支架、平衡環以及遙控器。最終，該公司在二〇一三年一月發布「大疆精靈」，這是第一款可以隨時起飛的預裝四旋翼飛行器：它在開箱一小時內就能飛行，而且第一次墜落不會造成解體。得益於簡潔和易用的特性，「大疆精靈」撬動了非專業無人機市場。

　　據說，汪滔還需要處理形形色色的商業間諜活動問題。他斷定過去兩年湧現出來的一些國內無人機創業公司曾非法獲取大疆的設計。

　　近幾年，大疆在海外開疆拓土，陸續設立了十七個辦事處，以輕量的辦事機構模式在各城市駐紮。具體來看，在日本有銷售和技術支持、在韓國有銷售辦公室、在德國和荷蘭有技術支持和物流支持、在北美好萊塢有銷售和市場、在帕羅奧圖有研發中心、在紐約也有辦公室。

　　在海外乃至全球的消費級無人機市場上，大疆可謂在終端制霸。從二〇一一年到二〇一五年，每年的營業收入在以三到五倍的速度增長，根據大疆方面的數據，二〇一五年達到六十億元銷售額，隨著基數的增大，二〇一六年相比二〇一五年銷售額增速放緩，上漲幅度在 60%-70%之間，以 65%換算，大疆二〇一六年銷售額約為 99 億元。

目前，大疆 80%以上的營業額來自海外，北美是最大市場，其次是歐洲，二〇一六年澳大利亞營業額增幅較大。

無人機變身辛勤勞動的農民

廣州極飛電子科技有限公司是廣東另一個名聲赫赫的無人機品牌。在極飛看來，無人機就是一位辛勤勞動的農民。她正在進入日本植保市場，與雅馬哈展開競技。

二〇一六年十一月，雅馬哈新款農業無人機 Fazer R 正式上市，售價為 1342.44 萬日元（約合人民幣 87.11 萬元），配備了燃油噴射發動機，可提供 20.6kW 的功率輸出；可在空中向著植物噴灑農藥，每次能噴灑農田近四公頃，最多可攜帶三十二升藥劑。同年十月，極飛也發布了該公司最新一款 P20 植保無人機、農業無人機飛控，並宣布推出植保無人機銷售和租賃業務。據瞭解，全新 P20 2017 款植保無人機系統包括無人機、GNSS RTK 定位設備（手持測繪器、移動基站、固定基站）、A2 智能手持終端、藥箱、灌藥機、智能電池和充電器，售價為 94999 元，裸機每架 48500 元。而普通用戶還可以選擇租賃 P20 植保無人機，租金則是按照作業量算。

成立於二〇〇七年的極飛自二〇一二年開始便研發農業植保無人機，在農業無人機領域取得了重大突破，獲得多項國家及國際技術專利。二〇一七年一月二十四日，極飛科技宣布成立日本子公司，正式在日本鋪開 P20 植保無人機銷售及植保服務網絡。

在極飛科技創始人彭斌的眼中，極飛的農業無人機通過在國內這麼多年的發展，在技術與生產製造上都擁有一定能力，甚至達到了一定的領先水平，進入日本市場是因為日本的農業跟中國面臨一樣的問題，那就是人口老齡化、勞動力成本急遽上升、農場人口減少等。但是這些問題在日本比中國更早到來，更需要這類自動化的農業無人機。

據英國《金融時報》報導，在日本以外很少人知道，自二十世紀八〇年代以來無人機就開始在日本的農田扮演重要角色，那時候摩托車生產商雅馬哈研發出了無人直升機，即用於噴灑農藥和播種糧食。日本家庭的餐桌上，每兩碗米飯中就有一碗是用雅馬哈無人機灌溉出來的。

在中國無人機領域，許多公司都選擇多向發展，但是極飛卻選擇了首先專注於農業這個相對「冷門」的領域。截至二〇一六年十月，極飛科技旗下的極飛農業已經組建了約八百人的服務團隊，在全國 14個省份的作業面積超過了二百萬畝，為近十萬用戶提供了無人機植保服務。並且在新疆和河南建立了極飛服務總站。

「我們其實探索過很多行業的運用，包括物流、警用、軍用等，但是在探索的過程中，我們最終選擇了農業。」彭斌說，農業的市場更廣闊，它可以給像極飛這類創業公司更好地施展拳腳的機會；另外，農業裡面有大量的空間可以用科技去改變，這也是極飛當初創業的目的，希望自己創造的產品或掌握的技能能夠解決某一項技術問題。

農業分為四個基本環節，在整個農業的生產週期中，耕地、種植、管理和收割是四個基本要素，而極飛參與的是管理環節。

「極飛通過兩條通道來服務農戶，第一條通道是極飛有一個自營團隊，可以給政府或大型農戶的種植土地提供噴灑服務，只要進行每畝多少錢的結算即可，例如每一畝地十元或十五元，不需要購買無人機;第二條通道,極飛有很多合作夥伴,他們可以給當地農場、種植戶提供服務。」彭斌說,「隨著農村土地越來越集中,土地流轉越來越快,越來越多的農場需要這樣的專業服務。未來農業一定是一個越來越分工細緻的行業。」

廣東高校
創客菁英

陳第：險象環生，步步為營的公司故事

　　華南理工大學二〇〇六級計算機專業畢業生陳第，在大學畢業三年後進入《福布斯》中文版「中國三十位三十歲以下創業者排行榜」。《福布斯》中文版對上榜者這樣評價：這些已表現出技術、產品和商業模式創新能力的青年人，已經具備很強的創業精神和顛覆能力。

　　在華南理工大學計算機科學與工程學院的師生眼中，讀書時候的陳第是個「技術控」「比賽控」。「我不喜歡做書面作業，但是並不代表我不愛學習。」陳第的好學不僅表現在他熱衷實踐、樂於動手實驗，更體現在他強烈的自學精神上。大二那年，為了跟隨曾經在全國挑戰杯上獲獎的師兄一起開發一項遊戲，陳第在完成課堂學習要求之外，幾乎天天泡在圖書館，鑽研更多的計算機技術知識，也幾乎每一天都是最後一個離開圖書館。

　　「華工的學術氛圍很自由、很開放，學院也鼓勵我們多動手，這些為我後來的創業選擇提供了很大幫助。」陳第說。也就是從大二那年開始，陳第陸續參加了「IBM主機應用創新大賽」「微軟菁英大挑戰」「全國大學生信息安全競賽」等大型比賽。「在學校的時候就能接觸這些著名企業，做一些實訓項目，對我的動手能力促進很大。」陳第很感謝母校為他提供了很多鍛鍊身手的機會，這些平台不僅讓他學習了如何進行項目管理、團隊合作，也讓他嘗試並確定了適合自己的發展方向，這一切都為他自己創業奠定了良好的基礎。

其實，出生於潮汕的陳第，從小就有著自己創業的夢想，自從參加各種比賽並小有收穫後，有種叫「天生的商業嗅覺」的東西就襲擊了他的大腦，他心裡開始反覆比較、思量，從大型機到 PC 市場，經過陳第不自覺的「商業風險評估」，他決定從手機小遊戲做起。

「年輕人覺得這個好玩，又是一個充滿機會的新興市場。」二○○七年的夏天，陳第跑去中華廣場那裡買來一部便宜的二手智能手機，和幾個同學編寫手機程序，當陳第發覺這些手機遊戲可以如此「酷炫」時，他乾脆拉了一幫熱愛技術的同學成立了工作室，開始天天貓在實驗室裡搗鼓各類手機應用軟件。藍牙三國殺、藍牙斗地主、3D 桌球……這些軟件被放在網絡上供免費下載，很快就有了每天兩千多次的下載量。但很快，陳第的團隊陷入了收費與否的窘境，面對開發者與用戶之間無法避免的矛盾，他說：「有些同學很享受編程的樂趣，但我更享受將技術轉化為生產力。我寧願花時間搞清楚如何做好一個產品把它商業化。」

大一的時候，陳第就做了一家類似攜程網的網站，但出現了兩個問題：與商戶簽約辛苦且效率低；流量太差導致業務很難開展。陳第讀的是計算機專業，他意識到創業的第一個教訓：一定要形成技術核心競爭力。

大二陳第開始研究技術創業，基本上形成了創始團隊的雛形。做了 IBM 的大型機項目，當時還想做全國信用系統。但現在想來對於一個初創團隊來講，這個項目很難商業化。當時這個項目拿了優秀應用獎，但沒有商業化。他當時還參加了一些微軟的比賽，主要是基於微軟的框架開發的一些遊戲和應用。在奧運期間，陳第來到北京微軟這裡實習，學到很多，「當時我意識到 PC 創業的時期已經過去了。」

二〇〇八年，陳第團隊參加了成都電子科技大學舉辦的全國大學生信息安全的大賽，提交了一個手機應用，那個應用的設計原理是記錄用戶輸入密碼時的解鎖力度，即使別人知道密碼但沒有掌握解鎖時的力度和節奏也不能打開。代碼很簡單量也很小，但評價相當高，還獲了二等獎。「這給了我們很大信心，覺得移動互聯網是可以創業的方向。」

二〇一〇年，即將畢業的陳第面臨著三個選擇：保送讀研、去新加坡參加交換生項目、自己創業。最後一個選擇似乎最不「靠譜」——輔導員希望他珍惜保研機會，團隊裡有人離開去了騰訊實習。「陳第，你創業我們就跟你創業，你讀研我們就一起讀研！」就在陳第糾結不知如何選擇的時候，兩位同班同學，也是他團隊一直以來的核心隊員李展鏗和張暖暉，堅定地宣布「同盟」。巧合的是，多年之後，人們把這一年稱為「移動互聯網元年」。

二〇一五年四月一日，有米五週歲。陳第在官網發布了有米移動廣告平台五週年的講話視頻。他激情洋溢地說，五年前，懷著讓「中國的智能手機開發者有飯吃」的樸素願望，有米作為中國第一家移動廣告平台成立了。最值得欣喜的就是，我們幫助了中國近萬的廣告主夥伴推廣其 APP 或手機網頁等產品，更幫助超過十萬的獨立開發者夥伴通過廣告獲得盈利，同時，累計促進全球超過十億用戶通過移動廣告參與到移動互聯網的信息傳播中。如今，創業團隊從最初的十來人發展到了三百六十多人；從廣州總部開始到北京、上海、香港等公司的設立，從中國市場走向國際市場！在接下來的幾年裡，互聯網金融、O2O、智能硬件、醫療和教育等各個行業與移動互聯網的緊密結合將成為這個小時代的突出亮點，有米將會積極參與其中，作為眾多產品服務的推廣者繼續發揮其價值，同時幫助更多的開發者、媒體，以及新興的內容創造者獲得盈利。

他也再次強調了「有米」名稱的內涵：大家有米，才是真的有米！

二〇一五年起，有米積極布局實施全球化戰略，建立專注於國際業務的全球化移動廣告平台 Adxmi。資料顯示，Adxmi 的廣告業務覆蓋 Android 與 IOS 雙平台，廣告流量遍布港澳台、東南亞（泰國、越南、印度尼西亞、菲律賓、馬來西亞）、北美、南美、歐洲等區域，覆蓋全球超過二百個國家和地區，與全球一千五百家媒介渠道有戰略合作關係。

米匯平台是有米除了「有米廣告+Adxmi」APP 廣告業務外，在社會化營銷板塊的又一重要布局。其定位是專注於社會化媒體的營銷平台。目前米匯平台已積累一千多個意見領袖，合作了超過十萬個微信行業公眾號，累計粉絲過億。

至此，有米已布局移動互聯網各流量入口，匯聚各方強勢資源，打造移動互聯網營銷生態圈。從公開資料來看，有米的營收規模、淨利潤、APP 覆蓋規模、終端覆蓋數量都屬於行業一線水平，其看準在長尾市場的發展優勢，拒絕了所有被併購，堅持獨立發展，立志做中國最大的獨立移動營銷平台。

當年，有米獲選二〇一五年《福布斯》中國最具潛力非上市公司 TOP10 以及二〇一五年中國最佳移動廣告平台。

二〇一六年三月四日，有米科技在新三板完成一筆總金額為2.5 億元的融資，讓陳第對新三板有了全新認識。他說，整個融資過程讓人感受到了新三板的魅力。融資更是超出預期，實際談融資時整個意向資金量達 4 億多元，如果當時（發布《股票發行方案》時）不把融資額度限制在 2.5 億元或以下，融資額可能會更高；融資效率也非常高，融資 2.5 億元僅用一個半月，不用跟 VC 一家一家談，效率提高很多。

對於未來的戰略，陳第描繪了「一橫多縱」的藍圖：有米以全球化的移動廣告平台作為「橫」線，將業務做廣；藉助移動廣告平台的優勢，重點布局遊戲、電商、金融、教育、O2O 等行業作為「縱」線，將業務做深，形成產業上下游的聚集，形成有米獨有的生態流量網絡。而對於移動廣告這條「橫」線本身，陳第對於有米發展戰略的初衷表現出堅定而強烈的信心：「我們服務的廣告主，最初很多都是 APP 廣告主，現在我們做了延伸，這些廣告主包含傳統的品牌，可能會推廣網頁、微信或者市場活動。此外開發者也做了相應的延伸，以前是中小 APP，現在是大的 APP，還有微信公眾號，包括自媒體號等等。」

王銳旭：向總理提建議的 九〇後 CEO

　　二〇一五年一月二十七日上午，中南海的一間會議室，國務院總理李克強主持召開科教文衛人士和基層群眾代表的座談會。王銳旭帶著發言稿、筆記本和筆，在工作人員的帶領下，到了中南海裡其中一間會議室。「每個人的座位早已安排好，而且座位前放著發言名單、發言順序等。」

　　王銳旭說，除了看到自己排在第七位發言之外，他才注意到自己是廣東地區的唯一代表，也是參會代表中最年輕的一個，與他一起出席會議的，還有姚明、陳道明、許寧生等，一共十人。

　　「直到那一刻，我才完全瞭解會議的內容：李克強總理主持召開座談會，聽取教育、科技、文化、衛生、體育界人士和基層群眾代表對《政府工作報告（徵求意見稿）》的意見和建議。」王銳旭說。

　　「坐下不久後，總理就走進會議室，微笑著跟每個參會代表握手。」王銳旭說，與總理見面握手的場景，雖然在心中早已排練過無數次，但當真正與總理握手介紹自己的時候，還是覺得非常緊張，手心也一直冒汗，「但依然能感受到總理的親和力」。

　　「輪到我發言的時候，緊張的心情已經平靜下來了。」王銳旭雖然準備了發言稿，但他發言的時候基本上是脫稿發言，「主要內容就是結合自身經歷對大學生創業提了建議，希望落實大學生創業扶持政策，為大學生創業者創造實現夢想的條件。」

「總理現場回應說，促進大眾創業、萬眾創新，大學生是其中的重要力量，要為他們實現夢想和自身價值『鋪路搭橋』、創造條件。」王銳旭說。

　　而在二月六日傍晚，王銳旭也在朋友圈轉發了一條題為《陳道明為何被總理邀請進中南海座談》的消息，並且留言稱「能和陳老師坐一席真幸福」。

　　「在一月二十七日晚上的《新聞聯播》播出大概五分鐘後，我們客服就收到一家媒體的電話，想要對我們進行採訪。在接下來的二十分鐘裡面，我們陸陸續續接到近十家媒體的約訪電話。」在王銳旭創辦的公司中擔任媒體推廣工作的 Ellen 說，「幾乎所有媒體都向我們提了這樣一個問題：王銳旭是憑藉什麼作為九〇後創業代表去北京參加座談會的？」

　　對此，兼職貓的創業團隊給出了「霸氣」的回應：沒有搶占朋友圈，也沒有高調秀融資，更沒有其他花邊新聞，比起狂妄、囂張、幼稚等這些給九〇後的標籤，相信大家更希望看到九〇後奮勇、堅韌、踏實、拚搏的一面，而王銳旭只是剛好做了一個表率，堅持做最努力最拚搏的九〇後創業青年。

　　參加總理的座談會後，王銳旭人氣爆棚，但他工作上基本沒什麼變化，似乎這幾天的事從未發生過。一月二十九日上午，他照常上班；下午，他出現在共青團與人大代表、政協委員面對面暨市政協十二屆四次會議提案交流會現場。王銳旭就建設一站式服務孵化基地建議：「希望孵化基地能夠建設得更具公益性，少一些商業元素，並且提供包括大學生政策申辦服務在內的一站式扶持服務。」

　　王銳旭剛剛從廣州中醫藥大學畢業才半年，他大三時創立的廣州九尾信息科技有限公司已順利拿下了第二輪天使投資和千萬級的A輪融資，公司估值過億元。但少有人想到，如今的年輕CEO是曾經的網癮少年，逆襲後在大學期間學業與事業共贏。從網癮少年、大學生創業者到總理的座上賓，他的歷程就是一本「勵志小說」。

確實，王銳旭有著不一般的「履歷」：除了在廣州中醫藥大學期間五次獲得獎學金，還曾經榮獲「中國優秀科普志願者」「千名志願者」稱號，獲得首屆廣州青年創意創業大賽一等獎、二〇一四「挑戰杯」廣東省創業實踐賽金獎、「粵港澳」移動互聯網設計大賽一等獎、校藥膳大賽一等獎等三十多個獎項，並獲創新創業訓練項目國家、省級立項各一項……他是學業與事業兩不誤的創業青年典型。

他的創業經歷更加非同一般，做的是手機應用APP，大學讀的卻是與此毫不搭邊的「中藥資源與開發專業」。他在創業前做過保安、擺地攤等兼職工作；大二成立魔燈團隊為企業進行校園品牌推廣；大三時用自己積攢的七萬元創辦九尾信息科技有限公司，組建了一個由十五人組成的創業團隊，主推「兼職貓」，供大學生在上面搜尋各種安全可靠的兼職信息。他曾用一份8角錢打印出來的兼職方案，贏得了創業的第一桶金。

讓人萬萬想不到的是，王銳旭曾是「網癮少年」。王銳旭出生在汕頭，家裡經營羊毛生意，開了廠房，他十一歲就在工廠幫父母「管賬」。上初中後，王銳旭成了網吧的常客，幾乎每天都要待上幾個小時，「有一次為了網遊通關，五一假期七天和弟弟泡在網吧裡，每人輪流打遊戲十二小時，甚至飯都顧不上吃。」王銳旭回憶，不久之後，自己成了不折不扣的問題少年，網遊、吸菸、喝酒、逃課樣樣均霑。禍不單行，中考前，家中工廠突遇危機，欠下巨額債務，家裡破產。初三畢業，王銳旭拿著二百八十分的中考成績單走到母親面前時，母親打了他一記響亮的耳光，「媽媽哭了，可以想像她有多傷心和無助。」王銳旭被拉回殘酷的現實，他開始意識到要挑起家裡的重擔。

於是他提出要接手父親的工廠，不料遭到父親的強烈反對。「他自己沒有文化，所以不想我們走他的老路。」王銳旭說。

王銳旭被送回初中復讀。父母也一改以往放養式的教育方式，加強對他學習的監督，為了幫助他戒掉網癮，特意把他送到附近沒有網吧的中學復讀。

王銳旭戒掉了網癮，埋頭苦讀，第二年考上了汕頭華僑中學，高考考上了廣州中醫藥大學。

大一時，王銳旭遇到心儀的女孩，因為談戀愛，生活費明顯不夠用，當打電話回家要生活費時，他聽出電話那頭母親的失望，家裡因破產依舊債台高築，「我骨子裡有潮汕的大男子主義，潛意識裡會想到要保護好母親，不能讓母親為我而傷心」。王銳旭痛下決心，要自己賺錢。一心找兼職的他卻先後遭遇了「交培訓費」「辦一百元的工卡」「交兼職服裝費」等五花八門的騙術，被黑中介騙走不少中介費。

在廣州中醫藥大學，王旭銳開始創業。他的辦公桌長一點五米，寬零點六米，在食堂靠東面，能坐下四個人。在這張桌子上，王銳旭「收復」了一個一個團隊成員，他們組建了魔燈團隊，和小夥伴們努力創業。「那時候，食堂阿姨對我笑笑，也是種莫大的鼓勵。」

委屈、白眼、苦頭、堅持、拚搏，換來了業務的上升，團隊人數也從「二人傳」升級為「四十人合唱團」，月收入也從零升到十五萬元。也是在這張桌子上，王銳旭開始了對未來的思考。在團隊發展的壓力下，出於對大學生兼職市場的耿耿於懷，王銳旭成立了九尾信息科技有限公司，並啟動了大學生兼職平台——兼職貓的開發。那時的資金並不足以支撐技術研發，於是除了技術團隊，所有人又投入了新一輪的校園代理和兼職工作中，只是為了一個簡單得不能再簡單的目的：養活技術團隊。

二〇一三年，他擁有了第二張桌子長二米，寬零點八米，有一部電話，有一台電腦，還有一群志同道合的創業青年。

它的位置坐落於白雲區一個創意產業園，是團市委專門為廣州青年就業創業發展提供的免費服務場地。

首屆廣州青年創意創業大賽，團市委邀請了一批專家和風投來「相馬」。作為一匹受人矚目的「黑馬」，王銳旭被相中了，不僅獲得創業大賽冠軍，還獲得一筆風投融資。

正是這些找兼職被騙的「慘痛經歷」，催生了王銳旭做「兼職貓」的念頭。也正因此，他創辦的「兼職貓」非常重視發布信息的真實性。而今，在王銳旭的帶領下，「兼職貓」的用戶已有百萬，並在前段時間順利拿下了第二輪天使投資和千萬級的 A 輪融資。面對互聯網激烈的「同質競爭」問題時，王銳旭自信地說：「這樣反而會更加激發大家的潛能，把這一領域做得更好。」

他表示，創業是為了賺錢，作為公司 CEO 的他有責任讓創業團隊過上好生活。「所以，不賺錢的創業都是耍流氓的」。

「作為從農村走出來的草根九〇後，我很珍惜。」王銳旭用行動給九〇後貼上了新標籤：奮勇、堅韌、踏實、拚搏。創業前期，作為團隊 CEO 的王銳旭需要全盤負責推廣、運營、公關等事務，「我的工作很雜，哪裡需要幫忙就過去幫忙，作為領導者要帶領大家」。而今，公司部門職能區分越來越清晰，團隊也不斷壯大，王銳旭主要負責統籌公司的工作。

　　王銳旭非常勤奮刻苦，基本每天從上午九點開始工作到晚上十二點，「好像一個人能做十個人的事，還經常幫忙做其他工作。」王銳旭在北京時因水土不服身體出現不適現象，但是第二天他依舊堅持上班、出席被邀請的會議。對此，他的解釋是：「我現在是創業者，就必須學會承擔這一身分帶來的所有責任。至於工作方面，我有身邊的夥伴陪伴著，和他們一起奮鬥，這讓我感覺很好」。

　　王銳旭表示，有關創業的活動，被邀請了，他一般都會參加。一月二十七日上午的座談會給王銳旭帶來了更多的目光，但是對他和他的團隊來說，低調做人，高調做事才是始終不變的原則。他一再提醒同事：要繼續努力，千萬不要驕傲，要踏實地做好產品。

蒲少濤：尿毒症逼我去創業

　　二〇一五年五月中旬，華南理工大學的基金會賬號收到二十萬元。看到捐款人姓名——蒲少濤，負責的老師有些吃驚。這位二〇〇五級的校友大二時被檢查出尿毒症，在學校和同學的幫助下，憑藉自強不息的毅力完成學業。他的病情維持治療花銷不菲，二十萬元從何而來？

　　二〇〇五年，蒲少濤從陝西農村考入華南理工大學，成為一名光榮的國防生，躊躇滿志之時，卻在二〇〇六年年底查出患有尿毒症。蒲少濤沒有怨天尤人，而是堅強面對病情。當時，無論是選擇換腎還是透析治療，數十萬元的醫療費對於蒲少濤和遠在偏僻鄉村的家庭而言，都是無法承受的。蒲少濤一直靠勤工助學自己掙生活費，為了省車費他甚至很少回家。在醫院接受治療期間，蒲少濤樂觀自信，為配合治療，他堅持一天只喝一口水，前前後後十餘次血液透析治療，每次都痛得全身直發抖，他從沒喊過一聲苦。學校的老師同學得知消息後，在他入院的第二天就籌到 3 萬多元捐款，隨後又多次組織募捐、義演、義賣活動：有的同學在飯堂義賣自己的美術作品，有的同學捐出自己整整半年的家教收入，有的同學自發組織策劃愛心義演，有的同學為他建立了一個網站，專門通告他的病情並呼籲救助……學校也成立了愛心基金，對他進行幫助。

　　經過一年多的治療，他的病基本好轉。出院後的蒲少濤重返學校，學校為蒲少濤提供了一間單人宿舍，他堅持每天四次、每次半小時的治療，每天起床後第一件事就是為自己進行透析治療，然後去上課，中午回到宿舍又接著做透析，下午下課後做第三次，晚上睡前還得再做一次。給傷口換藥、給房子消毒，按時打針吃藥也是他一手搞定。

未來看似黯淡，但蒲少濤並未自暴自棄，總是儘力做好力所能及的事。由於身體原因，蒲少濤不得不放棄國防生資格，課餘時間多了起來，他便自學鍾愛的計算機編程。「我得學個一技之長。」蒲少濤開始為自己考慮，於是選修了計算機專業的課程，還上網找教程學習。

如果那時有人經過蒲少濤的宿舍，經常可以看到他一邊做治療，一邊手敲鍵盤。「學編程的時候，感覺治療的時間過得飛快。」蒲少濤笑著說，學習也轉移了對治療壓力的注意力。

有一次，聽到老師說想找人將國防生網站改版，蒲少濤心頭一熱，便毛遂自薦。現在他做一個網站一個星期便能搞定，但當時由於技術不熟練，花了一個月的時間才把網站做出來。「硬著頭皮把作品交上去」，老師卻覺得新網站效果挺好。知道了蒲少濤網頁設計的技能，老師們熱情地介紹新的「客戶」給他，在校期間，蒲少濤給學校十幾個學院設計了網站，還接到些外校的單子。「兼職」幫蒲少濤賺取了一定的生活費，更重要的，是讓他增添了生活的自信心。

在二〇〇七年度「中國大學生自強之星」評選中，蒲少濤高票當選。

雖然獲取不小的榮譽，但強烈的生存危機還是擺在面前。蒲少濤對未來的期許是，找一份工作養活自己。他從未想過創業，直到面臨「畢業即失業」的尷尬。

二〇〇九年在金融危機掃蕩下，應屆畢業生面臨前所未有的艱難就業季。儘管如此，憑藉扎實的編程技術，有好幾個不錯的軟件開發類崗位向蒲少濤拋出橄欖枝。是否要隱瞞病情？蒲少濤在心裡掙扎過，最終還是選擇誠實告知。

　　一個公司打電話讓他去報到，他將病情告知對方，並再三保證：身體不影響工作，以後病情與公司無任何關係。但對方還是回絕了他。「我理解企業的做法。」蒲少濤嘆了一口氣說，「但看到其他同學都在討論找到的工作，心裡還是挺失落的。」至此，蒲少濤斷了找工作的念頭。

　　別人創業大多是出於興趣，或追逐理想，但對蒲少濤而言，創業是被迫無奈的選擇。恰在這時，學校老師給蒲少濤送來一個好消息：省裡正支持大學生自主創業，對於符合條件的學生可以提供一筆啟動資金。為此，蒲少濤拿到了十萬元的創業啟動資金。

　　畢業後，在與別人合租的民宅裡，「光桿司令」蒲少濤開始了網站設計與維護的創業項目。由於缺少資金，他一直在猶豫是否招人，「人來了沒項目怎麼辦呢」。但不邁出第一步，永遠不能獲得成功。最終，蒲少濤破釜沉舟般招了四名員工，搬進另一個一百四十平方米的民宅。壓力大，很多事情必須親力親為，蒲少濤的身體備受考驗。有一天晚上十點鐘，他給客戶送展板，回來時已經沒公交車了。那天天空下著大雨，他走了半個小時，腿都抽筋了。「經常為了幾百元的訂單熬夜」，蒲少濤很拼，因為他沒有退路。

　　一年多下來，去掉員工工資和各項投入，蒲少濤發現自己並沒有賺到錢。二〇一一年，聽從哥哥的建議，蒲少濤把目光投向了電商，成為天貓最早做建材與家居產品網上定製與銷售的商家。由於發展需要，他將創業戰場從廣州搬遷到了清遠，註冊成立了清新樂友家居用品有限公司，存儲倉庫從最初的一兩百平方米，擴大到一千多平方米，發展至今已成為一家專業的窗軌供應商。

隨著同類型網店越來越多，價格戰導致利潤降低，不利於公司長久發展。蒲少濤從營銷模式和服務質量突圍，希望成就「獨一無二」。公司在全國布局了線下服務網絡，「從廣州找一個師傅開始，半年時間新疆、西藏都有了人，只要訂單一下，師傅就上門進行窗簾的專業安裝服務」。

蒲少濤還開發了一套 ERP 系統，專門用於定製類訂單管理。早期用普通的網店銷售系統，客戶每改一個意見，就需要人工對照表格進行定價改動，效率低且容易出錯。改進系統後，大大減輕工作量，「之前得十五個銷售人員才能完成的工作，目前只需要十個人」。

為了更好地為顧客服務，公司還提出了「二十元規則」：即顧客收貨發現產品有不滿意之處（如顏色有差別），公司會給予買家幾元到二十元的賠償。因此，有的買家只是買了十元的產品，都有可能獲得二十元的賠償。

優質的產品與客戶體驗，蒲少濤的「致尚家居」旗艦店成為天貓窗簾配件銷售第一品牌。從二〇一二年開始，「致尚家居」已是天貓 KA 級商家。產品可以複製，服務可以模仿，公司要長久發展，轉型升級、掌握核心技術是關鍵。蒲少濤把目光轉向智能家居，嘗試通過手機控制整個家居的帶電產品，目前硬件設備正在測試。蒲少濤說：「如果可行，顧客回家前就可以通過手機 APP 先開好空調、放好洗澡水。」蒲少濤形容，「這就像給現在的產品裝上大腦。」

公司走上正軌後，蒲少濤以更加實在的方式回報社會。在粵北的清遠市，蒲少濤公司的員工大多數學歷不高，許多都是高中畢業生，但平均月收入能拿到四五千元，有些勤奮的甚至能拿到上萬元，「買房都不是難事」。每年公司會給員工安排體檢，也設立獎金獎勵優秀員工。另外，網店每一筆訂單成交額的千分之一，將會捐助給貧困山區小孩供其上學；蒲少濤還想為陝西農村的農產品打通網上銷售渠道，希望農民可以多掙一點錢。

終於攢到一些家產了，蒲少濤不聲不響地給華南理工大學基金會賬號匯款二十萬元，希望用於重病學生的幫扶。蒲少濤說：「在我最困難的時候，學校和社會給了我巨大的關愛和幫助，現在我有了一定的能力，要將這份關愛和幫助傳遞下去。」

工廠、村莊
遭遇互聯網

廠區新生途徑：
互聯網+！文化+！

隨著廠裡廣播的響起，工人們下班了。有師傅騎著自行車，載著老婆，去廠裡的菜市場買菜。有師傅端著陶瓷茶盅，穿著廠服，戴著白手套，準備去廠裡的小學接孩子放學。這是屬於二十世紀八〇年代廣州工業大道老工廠的記憶。

互聯網+紡織機械廠裡的微信總部

今天名震華南、微信總部所在的 TIT 創意園，前身是一九五六年成立的廣州紡織機械廠，也是當時華南地區最大的紡織機械廠。

今天，改造後的 TIT 創意園既有著老廠房的滄桑感，又帶著現代建築的冷峻時尚。從藝苑路的正門進入園區，十面長方形板牆按照冷色調到暖色調一字排開，方板中間鏤空出世界各地不同特色的服裝模特造型。園區之內，二十一座古樸的工業廠房、縱橫交錯的管道線網和和造型獨特的雕塑及工業機械模型，穿插在三百多株參天大樹之間，交織成別具一格的辦公空間。緋色斑斕的工廠磚牆上，印著帶有濃郁時代特色的壁畫及標語「工農群眾知識化，知識分子勞動化」，種種舊工業印記讓人像是回到了三十年前。

園區的服裝相關企業有十多家，其餘的企業則包括了網絡科技、影視傳媒、建築設計、餐飲酒吧等。其中，最知名的騰訊微信總部兩年前進駐，如今占據了超過五座廠房。

三三兩兩的員工在公司旁露天咖啡館開會，程序員們在電腦前瘋狂敲打著鍵盤⋯⋯這樣的情景在 TIT 並不鮮見。相比之下，服裝商鋪的生意顯得有些冷清。園區內的服裝企業大多走中高端路線，定位為「頂級」「定製」的高級服裝會所，服裝價格在八百至二千元。

廠區轉身，邁向電商產業園，城市的歷史記憶在這裡駐足，波瀾壯闊的二次創業史由此拉開。

地處廣州新中軸線南段的海珠區，在沿線形成了「廣州南中軸電子商務大道」，成為「互聯網+」主戰場。其中，廣一國際電子商務產業園正是從原廣州第一水泵廠廠房改造而來。該園區占地面積三點八萬平方米，重點入駐優秀大型企業總部、孵化優秀種子企業，享受海珠區電子商務有關扶持優惠政策，定位為建成文化與科技相融合的國家級電子商務示範園區，目前園區入駐企業四十五家，在孵企業十九家。

這樣的改造模式，既保留了「廣一」字號和風貌，更成為海珠區「退二進三」標誌性工程。

快速發展中的廣一電商園區雄心勃勃：計畫通過三年時間，改造修建創意辦公建築三萬至五萬平方米，引入三到五家知名的電子商務示範企業，集聚一百家中小電子商務企業。在園區實現年產值密度十萬元/平方米、納稅密度五千元/平方米以上，入駐企業年總產值超十億元，納稅一點五億元以上。運營方「五行集群」是電商、科技、創意園區開發、運營專業機構。有關負責人張民旭說，在廠區升級為電商園區的過程中，物理空間只是基礎，為總部企業、種子企業供應政務支持、創投、行業協作、創業氛圍這些服務

「催化劑」，創造企業易於成功的「化學空間」更為重要。

「比如一個企業，為什麼不在天河北、珠江新城的寫字樓辦公，要到園區辦公？租金是一個因素，員工的工作狀態、創意空間、創新社群，是更重要的部分。」

張民旭認為，老工廠轉型新電商園，必須深深植根所在地經濟升級和城市升級兩大土壤，真正實現從「物理空間」到「化學空間」的轉變。

文化+博物館引領，人民印刷廠正在設計最前沿產品

在「退二進三」戰略席捲廣州的同時，創意產業開始崛起。老工廠區開始昇華了。

作為「一個以國際標準定義的藝術、生活中心」紅專廠依然保存濃烈的工廠氣氛。現在，這裡有國內外知名的畫廊、設計工作室、藝術展示空間、時尚店鋪、特色餐廳及咖啡廳，這裡還有「休閒文藝的小清新」。文藝青年們充滿感情地寫道：「一個人的時候，你會愛上這裡。」

一九五六年，中國最大的罐頭廠「廣東罐頭廠」誕生於此。一九九四年，更名為「廣州鷹金錢企業集團公司」，在「退二進三」中，鷹金錢搬遷，藝術家們將廢棄的生產車間改造成了 LOFT 風格街區。

木板印刷的古畫、銅活字印刷的模型、兒時常見的油墨印刷設備、用鹽水就能發光的手電筒……位於燕子崗南路的廣州市人民印刷廠也是工業大道沿線的工業記憶之一。當印刷生產搬離海珠之後，這個老廠的招牌並未離去，靜靜變身成「包裝印刷文化創意產業園」，包括講述印刷歷史的廣州印刷博物館，防偽技術研發中心

和工業包裝設計研發基地。

有六十年歷史的廣州市人民印刷廠，對於不少廣州人來說都十分熟悉。當年的糧票、油票、債券、稅票、戶口簿就是在這裡印刷的。早些年開始，人民印刷廠已經悄然轉型，主要的印刷生產搬到了白雲區，而位於海珠區的老廠區，變身成為廣東省第一個印刷文化創意產業園。

走進印刷文化創意產業園，最吸引人的是這裡的廣州印刷博覽館。八百平方米的展覽館，原來是一個堆放印刷油墨和紙張的倉庫，現在則濃縮地展示了從甲骨文到最先進的數碼印刷的整個印刷歷史。在現場，不僅可以看到眾多木板印刷、活字印刷的實物，還有人現場演示唐朝最風行的雕版佛經印刷。

在現場還看到不少年代久遠的印刷機器，據人民印刷廠負責人介紹，這些都是過去人民印刷廠留下來的老機器。其中還有許多老一輩人都熟悉的油墨印刷設備——在一張蠟紙上刻字，然後用蘸了油墨的刷子一刷，墨就印到紙上變成文字。二十世紀七八十年代上學的人，小時候都做過這種油墨印刷的試卷。目前博物館申報愛國主義和科普教育基地。

而在博物館的二樓，則是現代最新的工業包裝設計理念的代表。展館中的一件展品很有趣，加進約三百毫升的淡鹽水，這個手電筒就可以發光一百個小時，「加海水甚至尿液都能使用，是應急的首選」設計者一邊演示一邊介紹這種具有專利的鹽水燈，一經推出就接到了日本的大量訂單，成為日本地震應急包中的必備品。

與工業包裝設計中心相鄰的是產業園的核心——防偽技術研發中心，目前已經研發出數十種防偽技術應用在包裝設計上。世界知名的惠普（HP）公司也在創意園內開設印刷品展示中心。

印刷博物館所在的創意產業園分三期進行改造，總占地面積一點零八萬平方米，總投資達到一點五億元。除了印刷博覽館，還形成高新技術研發區、文化創意設計區、專利技術孵化區、防偽技術應用中心，聚集一批與印刷相關的高新科技研發企業和文化創意企業、包裝設計企業。

舊記憶「工廠博物館」記錄廣州創業史

當電商園、創意園崛起，廣州輝煌的工業發展史卻並未被遺忘。

今年七十五歲的老工人黃師傅，常常會到創意園散步。他一九六八年進入廣州紡織機械廠工作，剛進入工廠時，廠房附近都是竹林，十分荒涼，「九〇年代中期是最輝煌的時候，全廠一千三百多名員工，一個廠長、九個副廠長，很多工人戲稱他們為『十大元帥』。」半個世紀的光景，這裡的英雄已經從「工廠元帥」變成了創意達人。黃師傅十分欣慰：「老廠倒閉關門之後，沒想到大部分廠房都被保留了下來。還記得我以前在供應科的廠房，現在變成了一家酒店。」

正在附近補習學校備考雅思的大學生小尚帶著北京的朋友專程來參觀 TIT，小尚的介紹簡單有力，「這就是廣州的 798。」在創意園北面，TIT 二期正如火如荼地建設著。

在工業大道中 313 號，大門處碩大的「東方紅」三個字似乎將人牽引回往日時光。東方紅印刷廠組建於一九六八年，二十世紀九〇年代起，新印刷企業遍地開花，那時候東方紅有「印刷的黃埔軍校」一說，吸引了很多人來做學徒。後來公司不景氣，有私企印刷廠跑來挖技術人員，只要穿著東方紅的工作服去面試，不用考試就可以通過。

二〇〇九年，東方紅關閉了印鐵車間，搬出廣州。現在拱門上的「東方紅」鮮豔醒目依舊，不過已經成為「東方紅創意園」的招牌。舊廠房被完整保留，磚牆上還殘留著種種標語，園區裡已經到處是攝影會所、網絡公司，還有讓人有些摸不著頭腦的「品牌疑難研究所」……老廠房變了，園區裡不再是統一制服的工人，而是慕名而來的遊客，奇裝異服的時裝模特。

曾經輝煌的廣州工業發展史打動著每一個造訪者。位於白鵝潭西岸、毓靈古橋旁的協同和機器廠在中國歷史上赫赫有名。一九一五年，這裡製造出中國第一台柴油機，扛起了中國近代民族工業的一面大旗。新中國成立後，這裡成為廣州柴油機廠的一部分。二〇一一年，這個百年老廠房退出了工業生產，變身為「柴油機博物館」，以老機器為背景展出當年工人們揮汗奮鬥的歷史場景。

隨著工業發展和更新換代，舊生產工具和資料被不斷淘汰。有心將其保存下來的，反而成就了今天的「工廠博物館」。

「淘寶」潮湧廣東農村

夜裡將近十二點，廣東揭陽市的軍埔村顯得十分安靜。在村裡著名的智慧大街上，多數網絡批發店早已關門，偶爾透過門縫能看到一些店裡包裝好的服裝碼得整整齊齊，堆積如山。作為省內最出名的淘寶村之一，二〇一六年的「雙十一」網購狂歡節，軍埔村電商銷售額超過了八千萬元。軍埔村電商的崛起，是廣東東區打造大軍埔電商圈的一環。從這裡流傳開去的發展經驗，正被廣泛複製到揭陽的城市和農村。

軍埔村位於揭東區錫場鎮，面積僅零點五三平方公里，現有家庭四百九十戶，二千八百多人。全村目前已有三百五十多戶近二千人投入網上銷售活動，開設各類網店三千多家、實體網批店三百二十多家。在這裡，基本上除了小孩和年紀太大的老人家，所有村民都在做電商，很多家庭主婦上了政府開設的免費電商培訓班之後，也開起了網店。現在已經很少有人知道軍埔曾是個社會矛盾突出的「問題村」。轉變源於三年前，幾名在廣州打工的本村年輕人返鄉開淘寶店創業。隨後引來無數村民效仿，軍埔村的人氣越來越旺，名氣越來越大，成為電商巨頭阿里巴巴認證的「淘寶村」之一。

目前，大軍埔電商圈已具雛形。軍埔電商模式作為一種可複製的經驗，已被揭陽市政府推廣到全市農村。

對，農村，這兩個字前所未有地和互聯網挨得這麼近！二〇一七年二月十五日，中國商務部就全國農產品市場體系建設情況發布信息：二〇一六年我國農產品電商交易額預計突破二千二百億元。

對廣東「村裡人」來說，這是一塊肥沃的新土地。在熱氣騰騰的「農產品電商」網絡末端，越來越多的鄉村小店成為電商企業的村級服務站，承擔著快遞包裹收寄、中轉的重要作用。

「一天至少有十來單貨。」廣東韶關始興縣太平鎮一家加入該網絡的村級服務站小店店主鄒婷婷在記者面前興高采烈。她說，現在的網購單子主要為家電、服裝和一些日用品，平時靠電動三輪車就可以送貨了，物流壓力並不大，而自己每月也有兩三千塊錢的提成。

二○一六年，廣東提出到二○二○年，全省農村電子商務應用水平顯著提高，農村電子商務支撐服務體系基本建立，城鄉產品雙向流通渠道基本形成，農產品網絡銷售及農村網絡購物規模持續擴大，整體發展水平居全國前列。在全省建成五十個縣級電子商務產業園和一百個鄉鎮電子商務運營中心，實現農村電子商務服務站在行政村全覆蓋。以電子商務、信息化及物流網絡為依託，以「萬村千鄉市場工程」為基礎，加快推進農村現代流通網絡建設，加強商貿流通、供銷、郵政等系統物流服務網絡和設施建設與銜接，暢通日用消費品下鄉進村渠道。

從農村考到城市的大學生們，也在竭盡所能，讓父老鄉親享受互聯網紅利。暨大的農村學生袁森林，大二暑假在梅州興寧調研時聽到一個小故事：一位在東莞上班的兒子特意為家鄉的老父親寄來了公司分發的粽子。但是鄉鎮間物流的不暢通，父親又很少接收郵件，這次快遞直接變成了「慢遞」。滿懷兒子心意的粽子送達父親手中時，已經變質不能食用。

袁森林和另外四名同在農村成長、在城市學習的「九○後」於是組隊立項，建設「鄉鎮通」平台。五個年輕人思想很一致：現階段農村物流和電商發展比較落後，農村的農產品難以運送到城市，城市的實用商品也難以運送到農村。他的團隊希望打造一個為農民提供電商服務來聯結農村人口和城鎮人口的物質紐帶。結合調研和所學知識，他們將「鄉鎮通」的服務分為鄉鎮物流代理和網絡平台代購兩個方面：在物流方面，將在縣城設置縣區總倉，統一代收快件，並與便利店合作，實現客戶自行到代理點取件；在代購方面，開發了農民導購平台，讓農民能夠「網購」。

這個小團隊開始為新年的「挑戰杯」全國大學生創業大賽做准備。從立項到參賽的兩年時間裡，「鄉鎮通」團隊為調研走遍了廣東省內如羅崗、葉塘等的二十多個鄉鎮。在汕尾市的一個農村，學生們遇到了一位老人。老人的兒女外出打工，常年不在家，家中地裡種植了龍眼樹。龍眼收購價格很低，再加上老人年事已高，家中大片的龍眼無人採摘，常常在樹上爛掉。袁森林的團隊徵得了老人的同意後採摘了一百斤的龍眼帶回深圳上網銷售，短短五十分鐘的時間，一百斤新鮮的龍眼被搶購一空。

「『龍眼』銷售體現的正是中國農村中普遍存在的一個問題：高質的農產品難以送達城市，造成的不只是農民的收入問題，還會導致資源的浪費。『鄉鎮通』的構想解決的就是『輸出』和『送達』的問題。」於是，作為中轉中心的快遞行業又成了「鄉鎮通」團隊調研的重點……

看好廣東農村電商事業的當然還有很多人。「農村電商是有前途的屌絲。」廣東亞太電子商務研究院院長陳海權在媒體面前如是評價。他說，廣東農村電商交易額保守估計二〇一七年能達到二百八十億元，二〇二〇年將達到四百三十億元。廣東有很多特色農產品，全省百分之八十五左右的縣已經形成花卉、蔬果、水產、肉類特色涉農產業。而且廣東不僅僅是農產品產量大，更是省外農產品重要的消費地和集散地。

▍城中村的互聯網夢想

二〇一六年九月二十三日，中國青年創業就業基金會與廣州市天河區政府簽訂戰略合作框架協議書，將在天河區的二十一個街道都建設五千至三萬平方米規模不等的中國青年創業社區。這也意味著全省首個中國青年創業社區「5ipark」將落戶廣州市天河區。

5ipark 互聯網青年創業社區是由五行孵化器集團、IDG資本、中國青年創業就業基金會聯合發起的互聯網孵化器品牌，她堅定選擇在廣東落戶，有著充足的理由。

共青團中央中國青年創業就業基金會秘書長陳宗雄心勃勃：「這是中國青年創業社區在全國首個與區級行政單位的合作項目，希望能在天河區做區一級行政單元合作的全國示範，未來可複製推廣」。他說，中國青年創業社區集創業賽事、創業培訓、創業服務、創業金融、創業社交、創業推廣和創業徵信於一體，為創業青年建造創業辦公、居住生活、休閒娛樂的創業「微城」，這一次首次落戶廣東省，選擇天河區為第一個站點，是因為天河區在 IT 產業、互聯網產業方面在全國具備領先優勢。與此同時，天河區一直在推動城中村孵化器建設，未來將拿出約四百萬平方米的城中村物業改造為眾創空間。

根據協議，雙方共同推進實施「中國青年創業社區及子品牌5ipark 互聯網青年創業社區」項目，在天河區推動及創建「一街道一社區」的示範發展模式，即在天河區二十一個街道中，力爭在每個街道建設五千至三萬平方米規模不等的青創社區，形成青年雙創孵化服務體系及青年創新創業人才庫，提供資源集中孵化，令各街道創業企業各具特色又互補，形成規模效應。

此外，每個青創社區都將劃出一定面積建設眾創空間，為創客群體提供全免費的工位及基礎孵化培育服務，力爭二年內在天河區實現三千個免費工位。雙方還將建立中國青年創業就業基金天河子基金，專項用於投資支持入駐青創社區雙創項目及團隊。

「5ipark 青創社區在天河區建設的範本，將建成集 5i 創新工場、5i 孵化器、5i 加速器、5i 創業公寓和 5i 創意街於一體的複合孵化器。」5ipark 互聯網青年創業社區聯合創始人張民旭說，5ipark 打造多種維度的社區文化體系，從多元化的社區組合、多樣性的城市新空間、地區及行業影響力強大的活動、專門的社員入社評審和服務、跨區域跨行業跨界的資源嫁接。「這不僅要構造一個耳目一新的社區空間，更重要的是要與入駐企業和人群一起，構造城市中更先進的工作和生活形態。」張民旭解釋，「5ipark 社區是盛行一時的眾創空間、創客空間的迭代產品，是創新型孵化器。」

在南粵都市，城中村們激發著越來越強烈的新創業夢想。在廣州中山大道西有一個棠下街，這是一個典型的城中村街道。七點四二平方公里分布了棠下、棠東兩個城中村，三十五萬人居住在此，其中外來打工人員就有二十六萬人，數量之多可居天河區城中村首位，日產垃圾二百三十噸，占天河區垃圾總量的六分之一。和廣州的大部分城中村近似，棠下街道路狹隘，崎嶇不平，轉角處隨處可見亂丟棄的垃圾，各類電線縱橫密布。

要讓這裡也能生長出孵化器，街道先後拆除南邊大街、大片路、東南路、三擔街、毓桂大街、官育路、口崗大街、豐樂路、富華街等街巷的占道梯級和鐵架，拓寬和新鋪瀝青路面近三千五百多米，修建人行道三千米，安裝交通欄四千二百米，疏通和新鋪一百五十條街巷下水道，解決二十六處長期困擾群眾出行的水浸街黑點；「微循環」管理模式也隨之引進，四條封閉式管理的車行道路使車輛能在村內按交通標志有序循環運行，五百多個高清攝像頭優化設置……有序的建設帶動當地物業的租金水平提高了百分之三十，同時也吸引了一批市場前景好、創新能力強的高科技企業進駐。棠下街用三個月的時間，重點對村公司現有物業周邊的環境進行集中整治，之後在棠下街轄棠東東路棠東村舊廠房園區，形成了一定規模的新三板孵化基地。

「村裡的眾創空間」建設現在還在天河持續推進。在全區約一千一百萬平方米的村集體物業中，拿出約三分之一改造為平價高效、設計新穎的創新發展空間。城中村的創新聚變效應正在顯現。天河區用較低的創業成本、較完善的創業創新服務鏈條，對數以萬計的創新創業者敞開懷抱。同時，天河區城中村的村民從原先出租物業謀生到加入新經濟大潮，一些村集體經濟組織甚至參與到互聯網生態家園項目的投資中，成為全球創新鏈的一環。

明文庫‧悅讀中國 A0607033

中國夢‧廣東故事——創新的廣東

者	陳 翔
權策畫	李煥芹
主編輯	呂玉姍
行 人	陳滿銘
經 理	梁錦興
編 輯	陳滿銘
總編輯	張晏瑞
輯 所	萬卷樓圖書股份有限公司
版	菩薩蠻數位文化有限公司
刷	百通科技股份有限公司
面設計	菩薩蠻數位文化有限公司
版	昌明文化有限公司

園市龜山區中原街 32 號

話 (02)23216565

行 萬卷樓圖書股份有限公司

北市羅斯福路二段 41 號 6 樓之 3

話 (02)23216565

真 (02)23218698

郵 SERVICE@WANJUAN.COM.TW

垚經銷

明外圖臺灣書店有限公司

電郵 JKB188@188.COM

N 978-986-496-399-7

9 年 3 月初版

賈：新臺幣 300 元

如何購買本書：

1. 轉帳購書，請透過以下帳戶
   合作金庫銀行 古亭分行
   戶名：萬卷樓圖書股份有限公司
   帳號：0877717092596

2. 網路購書，請透過萬卷樓網站
   網址 WWW.WANJUAN.COM.TW

大量購書，請直接聯繫我們，將有專人為您
服務。客服：(02)23216565 分機 610

如有缺頁、破損或裝訂錯誤，請寄回更換

國家圖書館出版品預行編目資料

中國夢.廣東故事——創新的廣東 / 陳翔著. --
初版. -- 桃園市：昌明文化出版；臺北市：
萬卷樓發行, 2019.03
　冊；　公分
ISBN 978-986-496-399-7(平裝)

1.區域研究 2.廣東省

673.3   108002849